tunnels!

•••

true stories from the edge

true stories from the edge

Diane Swanson

tunnels!

ANNICK PRESS

TORONTO + NEW YORK + VANCOUVER

Annick Press Ltd.

We acknowledge the support of the Canada Council for the Arts, the Ontario Arts Council, and the Government of Canada through the Book Publishing Industry Development Program (BPIDP) for our publishing activities.

The author gratefully acknowledges the support of the British Columbia Arts Council.

Editing by Pam Robertson
Copy-editing by Elizabeth McLean
Cover and interior design by Irvin Cheung/iCheung Design
Cover illustration by Michael Downs
Interior diagrams by Stephen MacEachern

Cataloging in Publication Data

Swanson, Diane, 1944–
    Tunnels! / written by Diane Swanson.

(True stories from the edge)
Includes index.
ISBN 1-55037-781-7 (bound).--ISBN 1-55037-780-9 (pbk.)

    1. Tunnels--Juvenile literature. I. Title. II. Series.

TA807.S83 2003   j624.1'93   C2002-904770-6

Distributed in Canada by	Distributed in the U.S.A. by	Published in the U.S.A. by
Firefly Books Ltd.	Firefly Books (U.S.) Inc.	Annick Press (U.S.) Ltd.
3680 Victoria Park Avenue	P.O. Box 1338	
Willowdale, ON	Ellicott Station	
M2H 3K1	Buffalo, NY 14205	

Printed and bound in Canada

Visit us at **www.annickpress.com**

Contents

A Note from the Author

Tugging hard, my friend and I struggled to unstick a deep drawer built into an attic wall in her rambling, old home. All we wanted was the board game stored inside. But with our final yank, the whole drawer fell out—exposing a gaping hole behind it.

As we poked our heads through the opening, we could just make out a narrow passageway. It barely seemed big enough for us to wriggle through—but we did. Heads down and arms pressed against our sides, we wormed our way through the short tunnel. Much to our surprise, we ended up in a large room.

Slivers of light slipped through narrow gaps between the upper boards of one wall, revealing nothing. Only layers of dust. The "room" was probably just dead space between the surrounding rooms that the previous homeowner had built in the attic. Still, to a pair of nine-year-olds with active imaginations, it was a thrilling discovery: our very own hideaway with a secret tunnel entrance.

Ten years later, I had a chance to explore a second tunnel. This one sat deep underground in a coal mine. With two friends and an experienced miner to guide us, I stepped eagerly into the elevator that took us straight to the bottom level.

Midway along the lowest passage, the miner told us to turn

off the battery-powered lamps on our hard hats. At the click of a switch, we were instantly plunged into an inky blackness. I could scarcely believe that I was able to touch my forehead without catching sight of my hand. Never before had I experienced the wonder—and terror—of absolute darkness. It was an electrifying moment.

When I set out to write this book, memories of my brief experiences inside tunnels came flooding back. They inspired me to learn about some of the many tunnel dramas from around the world. And they reminded me that I would uncover varying accounts of what really happened. Just as my friends do not remember our shared tunnel experiences exactly the way I do, people everywhere tell differing stories about the same events. No two persons store and recall identical memories of anything. As well, everyone's recollections change over time.

Author Diane Swanson (right) at age 19 with two friends, after exploring an underground tunnel in a coal mine.

In researching the dramas in this book, I sometimes discovered major discrepancies. Several prisoners of war, for example, reported the digging of a tunnel at night, but some of their fellow captives claimed it was built during the day—while outfoxing the guards. Accounts of other stories varied in less important ways. Was the clue that led East German soldiers to the entrance of a hidden escape tunnel a carelessly abandoned baby stroller or a toddler's wagon?

As an author, I consulted a variety of sources, then wrote what I could verify best. But regardless of the variation among reports, these dramas from the underground are all very real. Further, the courage and ingenuity of the people involved seemed to remain clear in everybody's mind.

One moonless night in Wisconsin, two hunched figures slipped silently into a log cabin. They raised a trapdoor in the floor and disappeared underground. Bending low, they crept about 12 m (40 ft.) through a narrow dirt tunnel no more than 1.5 m (5 ft.) high. When they reached the basement of a stagecoach inn called Milton House, they collapsed with relief.

The year was 1851. The Underground Railroad—a secret support network for runaway slaves—was thriving, despite a law that required Americans to help recapture escapees. In the basement of Milton House, owner Joseph Goodrich not only hid runaway slaves, he gave them food and protection. At his inn, they had a chance to rest up for the next stage of their daring escape, often heading north to Canada. When the time was right, they would make their way back out through the tunnel, one of few parts of the Underground Railroad that was actually underground.

Tunnels for All Reasons

People have been tunneling since the Stone Age, when they first scraped through rock to enlarge their caves. Since then, they've built tunnels for every reason: hiding slaves, escaping heat, fleeing prisons, launching attacks, robbing banks, burying bodies, drawing water, finding treasure, mining ore, rescuing hostages, smuggling goods, and creating routes for traffic. They've burrowed through mountains, under rivers, beneath deserts, and below cities. They've dug deep into the bowels of Earth and high up where the air is almost too thin to breathe. And they've persisted in the face of life-threatening risks from cave-ins, floods, and toxic gases.

Of all the many kinds of tunnels in the world, the most common are those that lie under cities—tunnels that bring in water, cart off sewage, deliver gas, and carry lines for electricity, telephone, and cable. Beneath New York City alone, there are more than 51 million km (32 million mi.) of service lines. And the number and size of tunnels grow with the city. Since 1970, crews have been working on an enormous new water tunnel for New Yorkers, and they're not finished yet. It's a project so huge it will likely take 50 years to complete.

Beneath cities, there are also some bizarre uses for tunnels. Under the Russian capital of Moscow are large tanks of preserved sea creatures—stored for the Academy of Oceanology—and passageways with stone altars where people in robes carry torches and sing. Moscow's tunnel explorers even found a torture chamber. Ivan IV, czar of Russia in the 1500s, had set up a maze of underground passages and rooms where he enjoyed watching wild animals eat people. He wasn't called "Ivan the Terrible" for nothing.

In England, a kindhearted man named Joseph Williamson built tunnels nobody needed because he believed everyone deserved the chance to earn a living. From 1805 until his death in 1840, he spent his life's fortune hiring men who couldn't find jobs in Liverpool. Williamson organized make-work projects, paying men to build tunnels to join the cellars of the houses he owned. He commissioned some passages that went nowhere special, and sometimes assigned work crews to close up tunnels that other crews had just finished building.

Although most of the men Williamson hired were unskilled, many developed a trade—bricklaying or stonemasonry on the job. Eventually, they were able to find "real" work elsewhere.

Shelters for the Living...

Some people make their homes—temporary and permanent—in tunnels beneath cities. Their doorways are simply grates in roads. The lucky ones have jobs, so they come and go each day, sometimes managing to add a few luxuries, such as radios, to their underground shelters. Many others live in total poverty, and most risk picking up diseases from the filth that collects in tunnels. They also have to face tough gangs who frequently patrol the dark underworld.

Coober Pedy is different, though. It's a small mining town in Australia's dry central region, called the Outback. Summer temperatures there soar to 45°C (113°F) in the shade and dust storms blast through the streets. Thick swarms of flies force residents to do the "Outback salute," waving their hands around wildly to keep the insects out of their ears, eyes, and noses. But since 1915, when teenager Willie Hutchinson tripped over some valuable rocks called opals, miners and their families have settled in Coober Pedy.

To escape the harsh conditions of the Outback, many residents tunneled out large homes in the sides of hills. Some of them even boast indoor swimming pools. Today, about half the town's 3,500 people live in these fancy "dugouts."

Coober Pedy also has underground stores, restaurants, and churches. Its name, which means "white man in a hole," reflects the town's dugout lifestyle. As the story goes, Aboriginal people who noticed opal miners tunneling into the sandstone called the spot "kupa piti." English-speaking tongues twisted that into Coober Pedy.

...Tombs for the Dead

Most people who inhabit tunnels are dead, not alive. Many rest in underground burial sites called catacombs that lie beneath several of the world's great cities. In Paris, France, catacombs hold the remains of millions. Their skulls and other bones are stacked along the walls of damp, narrow passages in areas once mined for rock to build the city. When cemeteries in Paris became overcrowded in the 1700s and 1800s, the bones were shifted to the catacombs.

Today, a few of the hundreds of kilometers of catacomb passageways are open to visitors. At the official entrance, there's a notice that reads: "Stop. This is the empire of death." Yet the site attracts thousands.

Of course, sneaking into the catacombs through street vents is discouraged as it's easy to get lost in the maze of passages. Guides are quick to point out that one man went missing for 11 years before turning up—dead. He was then buried in the catacombs.

Spying from Below

Keeping a hidden eye and ear on the enemy is a practice as old as time. And it's sometimes done from the dark privacy of an underground tunnel. Spying often goes undiscovered, but in the spring of 2001, one possible episode came to light with the arrest of a double agent in the United States. Robert Hanssen, who had been working as a spy for the Federal Bureau of Investigation (FBI), was caught selling American security secrets to Russia. One of those secrets supposedly revealed the existence of a spy tunnel beneath the Soviet Embassy—now the Russian Embassy—in Washington, D.C.

Such a tunnel would have allowed American agents to eavesdrop on the embassy during the 1980s and 1990s. They might have used high-tech spying equipment, such as laser beams that detect vibrations from the keystrokes of machines sending coded signals. But if Soviet officials knew about a tunnel, their communications would surely have been either "empty" or loaded with misinformation.

The American government has never confirmed the existence of the Washington spy tunnel.

Streams of Life

Not all unusual tunnels are the stuff of spy plots and creepy catacombs. Some simply support the struggle to live. In 1844, missionary William Philip and his congregation of Khoisan farmers built South Africa's first irrigation tunnel. Using the simplest of hand tools—pickaxes, hammers, and chisels—they labored for more than a year to cut through a mountain of solid rock. They hauled the pieces off in baskets until they had created a passageway that stretched 102 m (334 ft.)—long enough to divert river water to the land they wanted to farm.

For more than 1,000 years, the people of Bali, Indonesia, have cut tunnels through rock to tap water from mountain streams. They channel it through a system of aqueducts and bamboo stalks to the top of their terraced land. From there, the water flows downward, falling from farmer's field to farmer's field and giving life to crops of rice, the primary food for most Balinese.

The people of Afghanistan have channeled water through tunnels for more than 2,000 years. Many of their rivers dried up during hot seasons, so farmers in parts of the country built a vast network of underground tunnels. In the Afghan foothills, they dug shafts—some more than 30 m (100 ft.) deep—to reach ground water. The shafts connected with the network of tunnels, letting water flow across the desert. When it reached towns and villages, it poured into irrigation ditches and onto fields, making farming possible.

War and the Underground

The Afghan system of underground water tunnels has also been used to escape enemies such as Genghis Khan, the formidable 13th-century Mongol invader. And from 1979 to 1989, villagers and local armies hid from invading Soviet soldiers by disappearing into the tunnels closest to their towns. Unseen, they traveled through the network from one place to another. They also dug holes into the sides of water shafts, where they could hide, store weapons, and launch attacks.

It's no wonder that world terrorist Osama bin Laden, who

set up camps in Afghanistan to train his followers, used this vast tunnel system, too. In 2001, when armed forces from several nations, including Afghanistan, attacked the terrorists, they fled to the country's tunnels and natural caves to escape and return fire.

Although some tunnels have served more than one purpose, others have been built only to support warfare. Germany even built underground passageways on Guernsey, one of the Channel Islands and the only British land occupied by Germans during the Second World War. Dictator Adolf Hitler moved his soldiers to the island to form part of an "Atlantic Wall" that would help hold back his enemies.

The Germans forced hundreds of laborers—including Russian and Polish prisoners of war—to dig tunnels out of the solid rock on Guernsey. The workers slaved long hours with very little to eat. Some of them died from the labor and are believed to be buried in the tunnel concrete. But despite such losses, the Germans had constructed 29 tunnels on the island by the end of the war. The largest held a military hospital with wards for injured soldiers, operating theaters, an X-ray room, a cinema, and a mortuary for the dead.

Sneaking Out

During World War II, the German army also played a role in one of the most famous escape dramas of all time. The Germans ran a prisoner-of-war (POW) camp, called Stalag Luft III, which they thought was escape-proof. But in 1944, 76 POWs crawled through a trapdoor under a stove and out through a long, narrow tunnel they had secretly dug beneath the camp.

Only three of the POWs made their way to freedom. The others were recaptured and either taken back to the camp or shot to death on Hitler's orders. Still, the tunnel they had created—right under the noses of the German guards—was nothing less than amazing.

Not all such tunnels have been built for mass escapes. Many were created so that just one person could flee—a prisoner kept in a jail cell or a victim held by a kidnapper. Former Peruvian spy chief Vladimiro Montesinos used an escape tunnel to vanish from his luxury beach house in October 2000. Wanted on charges of theft and torture, he had a $5-million reward on his head. When investigators searched his home, they found a trapdoor under his pink bathtub and another by his indoor swimming pool. Both doors opened into a tunnel that ran under his property to a hatch inside the garage of a neighboring house.

Montesinos's bodyguards claimed that the trickster fled Peru on his yacht, *Karisma*. He simply slipped away among sailboats that were taking part in a race to Ecuador. Once all the boats were out at sea, he made his escape, unnoticed.

Art, Adventure, and Tall, Tall Tales

Even if their original purposes were practical, tunnels aren't always put to serious uses, such as carting water, burying bodies, or running away. Along one wall in a passageway beneath the Organization of American States building in Washington, D.C., there's a painting that's more than 162 m (532 ft.) long. The artist, Carlos Paez Vilaro, created the longest mural in the world. He painted the semi-abstract *Roots of Peace* in 1960 with help from students attending the Corcoran School of Art and the

University of Maryland. They worked for four weeks, brushing 400 kg (880 lb.) of paint on the wall.

In 1998, a father and son foolishly used an abandoned gold mine in California for an adventure in climbing. They were 120 m (390 ft.) down a steep shaft when they decided to return to the surface. As they were climbing back up, the father fell 15 m (50 feet) and landed on a ledge below. His rescue took more than seven hours and the help of 70 people. The man survived—unlike many adventurers in abandoned mines. Sometimes, not even their corpses are recovered.

On the Canadian prairies, Moose Jaw, Saskatchewan, draws thousands of visitors to its underground. Remnants of passageways between the basements of old buildings have inspired many rumors. There are tales of Chinese immigrants escaping racist hysteria and of bootleggers smuggling alcohol into Moose Jaw during the "dry" early 1900s. There are even stories of big-time gangster Al Capone hiding out in the tunnels. No one really knows who built the passageways, how they were used, or how many exist. But that hasn't stopped people from guessing or even building new tunnels to represent the ones they believe are there.

Reports of ghosts can add to the attraction of tunnels. Visitors to central England hope to spot the phantom of an old lady in two canal tunnels that boats pass through. The spirit of Kit Crewbucket, who was murdered and dumped in the water in the 1800s, supposedly haunts the passageways today.

Boatmen at Crick Tunnel claim Kit is a friendly ghost who sometimes cooks breakfast on board for crews that she fancies. But at Harecastle Tunnel, she has a much darker reputation.

Her ghost is said to appear headless as a warning that someone will soon drown. In the 19th century, horrified boatmen often took long detours to avoid passing through Harecastle Tunnel.

Ten Dramas More

Every country has its tunnels, from the famous spiral tunnels along Canada's railroad in the rugged Rocky Mountains to the amazing Chunnel that links England and France beneath the English Channel. And every one of them has a story to tell.

The rest of this book focuses on 10 dramas—from around the world—in which tunnels have played leading roles. There are stories of fighting the Vietnam War, fleeing East Germany beneath the Berlin Wall, freeing hostages in Peru, surviving a mining disaster in Canada, and escaping from an American Civil War prison. Some of the stories are about crooks, who robbed a bank in France and smuggled drugs from Mexico. Other stories concern heroes, who fought a fire near Italy, dove into a flooded tunnel in Britain, and discovered the ancient tomb of Egypt's King Tutankhamun. Extraordinary dramas. All underground. All true.

DA, DA. RATTA-TAT-TAT. DA, DA, DA-DUM. March after march blared from loudspeakers near an embassy in Lima, Peru, the amplifiers set at full volume. Military tanks roared up and down the surrounding streets, while low-flying helicopters clamored noisily overhead. The racket was deafening. But then, that was the whole idea. Drown out the sounds of miners at work, busily tunneling under the street...below the garden...beneath the mansion. Drown out the sounds of a daring rescue in progress.

Happy Birthday!

It all began with a lavish party on December 17, 1996. Japan's ambassador to Peru, Morihisa Aoki, was hosting a gala celebration to honor his emperor's 63rd birthday. More than 1,000 invitations had been delivered to Lima's elite, such as Alberto Fujimori, the president of Peru. Fortunately for him, he did not attend, but members of his family did: mother Rosa, sister Juana, and brother Pedro. They were among the approximately 450 guests who arrived at the Japanese embassy that night.

Ambassadors from other countries, such as Bolivia, Canada, Germany, and Greece, attended the party. So did several Japanese business executives and many Peruvian government leaders, judges, professors, generals, and top-level police officers. Peru's director of anti-terrorism was also there.

The embassy was a roomy mansion that had been modeled after Tara, the stately southern home of Scarlett O'Hara in the American Civil War novel and movie, *Gone With the Wind*. To make the building secure, the doors were built to withstand the force of exploding grenades. Grates had been installed on all the windows—even those made of bulletproof glass. As well, a tall wall surrounded the embassy property.

Although the mansion was spacious, Aoki had so many guests that he held the birthday reception beneath a huge tent in the back garden. After all, December is summertime in Peru.

The party began as an elegant affair: dressy people sipping glasses of bubbly champagne and nibbling on dainty appetizers. But at 8:30 p.m., all that changed. Without warning, rebels blew a hole through the wall from the neighboring property and charged into the embassy grounds. They were packing machine guns and grenades. Some of the "waiters" who had been serving champagne immediately pulled out guns and joined the takeover.

Stunned into silence, the party guests dropped to the ground. One of them reported hearing a rebel yell, "Don't lift your head, or it'll be shot off."

Embassy staff reacted swiftly, but some were gunned down. Security—both inside and out—had been relatively light that night. Officials believed that Peru had largely defeated the rebel troops who were fighting to establish a communist-style government. The police and armed forces had relaxed their guard—too soon.

The rebels took everyone at the birthday celebration hostage, and almost at once, police officers surrounded the embassy grounds. They hurled canisters of tear gas, but only the party guests choked. The rebels pulled gas masks over their faces and won the skirmish easily.

Rebels with a Cause

Surprisingly, the successful seizure of the entire embassy—and everybody in it—had been achieved by only 14 people, mostly teenagers. Their leader, however, was a very experienced rebel. As a young man, 43-year-old Nestor Cerpa had organized a labor protest in a textile company and had taken hostages there. He had served time in jail for his actions. And in 1984, he had helped form the *Movimiento Revolucionario Tupac Amaru* (MRTA), the Tupac Amaru Revolutionary Movement. It was named after brave Incan rebels who fought against Spanish control of their country in both the 16th and 18th centuries.

In their efforts to bring communism to Peru, the Tupac Amaru had adopted a hard-line approach. They had stopped short of nothing—bombings, kidnappings, and slayings—in the name of their cause.

The response from Peruvian officials had been almost as tough. They had jailed thousands of MRTA members and supporters. More recently, they had captured the movement's leader and Cerpa's own wife, Nancy. Living conditions for these political prisoners were harsh. They reportedly survived only by killing and eating rats. "Slow-death penalties" was how some people described their jail sentences.

After taking control of the Japanese embassy, Cerpa and

his gang demanded the release of approximately 400 imprisoned MRTA rebels, including Nancy, in exchange for the hostages. They insisted that the government provide transportation for the released prisoners, the hostages, and themselves to a jungle hideout, where the hostages would be released.

Standoff!

President Fujimori's sharp reply to the demands of the Tupac Amaru was clear: "NO!" So the rebels dug in their heels. They planned to wear down the government's tough position by standing guard in the embassy. After all, the fortresslike mansion was easy to defend from the inside, and the rebels were heavily armed with rifles, grenades, antitank guns, and automatic weapons. Cerpa told one hostage: "We came physically and mentally prepared to stay for a long time."

Still, the rebels couldn't manage such a huge group of people. Within hours, they began releasing some of the hostages, mainly the elderly and the women, including Fujimori's mother and sister. And over the first few weeks of the standoff, they freed many others—as well as Emma, one of Aoki's pet dogs. But they held onto 72 people: Peruvian officials, Japanese dignitaries, and the Bolivian ambassador. Also among the remaining hostages was a courageous priest who could have left, but who asked to stay to support his companions.

The actions of the MRTA didn't go unnoticed by the media. The Peruvian rebels' fast, well-organized attack on foreign soil—the Japanese embassy—was one of the most dramatic actions ever taken by the Tupac Amaru. In fact, it was one of the boldest hostage-grabbing efforts on record, anywhere.

What's more, the captives were all powerful people. The eyes of the world were focused on Lima, Peru, and the attention pleased Cerpa and his gang.

President Fujimori appeared to try to cut a deal with the MRTA. He appointed negotiators, and at one point offered to let the rebels escape to Cuba—without any of the hostages. Secretly, however, he focused on developing a plot to rescue the captives from the embassy.

Life in the Embassy

In the early days of the crisis, there were so many hostages crammed into each room they felt short of air. Summer's heat was made more intense by the rebels, who barricaded the windows with furniture, shutting out any breeze.

During cool nights, there weren't enough blankets to go around. Nor could the hostages all find floor space to lie down. Instead, they tried to sleep crouched over. To make matters worse, their overused toilets frequently backed up.

Ambassador Aoki blamed himself for the lack of security that allowed such a crisis to occur. Every day, he spoke to each of the other hostages, apologizing and offering whatever he had to make them more comfortable.

After some of the hostages were set free, the 72 who remained were less cramped, but they felt uneasy—to say the least. They wondered what would become of them. Many never expected to get out of the mansion alive. But week by week, life in the embassy became more brain-numbing than it was frightening. Time dragged, and boredom smothered terror.

Most mornings, the captives awoke to the chants and

military drills of the Tupac Amaru. Then they did chores, such as sweeping floors. They tried to exercise, jogging along corridors and up and down staircases. To keep their minds busy, they read and played chess, and took turns giving talks on whatever subjects they knew well. And the Peruvian hostages helped the Japanese improve their Spanish.

Bedtime came early, as the government had shut off all power to the embassy. During the long, dark nights, the captives lay listening to rats scampering around the rooms and inside the walls.

Fortunately, Red Cross workers were allowed to bring in food, water, clothing, and thin foam mattresses. Sometimes they delivered letters from families. And they tended to the sick.

On most days, Cerpa treated the hostages with polite respect. The other rebels were occasionally cruel, threatening the captives with guns. The worst was one of Cerpa's senior lieutenants, who always kept two grenades hanging from his neck. He seemed to enjoy horrifying the hostages with the details of how he had murdered police officers.

As more weeks passed, the Tupac Amaru, like the hostages, grew discouraged and bored. To help pass the time, most of the rebels, including Cerpa and his three lieutenants, played indoor soccer on the main floor. For about an hour every afternoon, they set their weapons aside and kicked around a taped ball they had made out of rolled-up cloth. The other rebels either watched from their lookout positions or took light naps.

By the middle of March, Cerpa began to suspect that the Peruvian military might be trying to tunnel into the embassy. He didn't appear to have any contacts outside the building who might help him discover what was happening. But, being cautious, he moved 36 hostages up to the second floor, crowding them into eight bedrooms with the 36 already there.

Then Cerpa and his gang took positions along the upper hallway. They often aimed their rifles into the rooms, sometimes pretending to toss in grenades. "If we're attacked," Cerpa warned, "nobody here will survive!"

The rebels were most alert during the nighttime, when they watched and listened closely for any sign of a raid. Cerpa sometimes slept in the hostages' rooms. The other rebels policed the hallways. They kept a special eye on Pedro Fujimori, the president's brother, frequently shoving loaded guns close to his face.

As time went by, Cerpa grew more wary and hostile. Even his demand for the release of just 20 MRTA prisoners—down from 400—was rejected. When the rebels and hostages went to sleep each night, they were unsure they would ever wake up.

The Plan

While all this was going on, President Fujimori, Peru's National Intelligence Service, senior police officers, and the Peruvian armed forces were working out an elaborate plan to get the hostages out of the embassy alive. They figured that if they tried to storm the mansion either by air or by land, the MRTA would have time to shoot the captives. A surprise attack from underground seemed the only reasonable approach, but the plan would have to be kept highly secret.

The planning team came up with two operations. One was phony; the other, real. Operation Freedom was made public. Reporters were invited to photograph soldiers supposedly being trained for an assault on the embassy. Well-armed troops and military trucks and tanks circled the grounds, while helicopters passed overhead. The police played loud, patriotic marches all day long.

With its noisy show of force, Operation Freedom unsettled the rebels. It also interrupted the sleep of those who had to rest in shifts. But its main purpose was to cover up the real rescue plan: Operation Chavin de Huantar. That plan was named after an ancient civilization that had been especially skilled in tunnel-building. President Fujimori had recently visited an old temple at the Chavin de Huantar site in northern Peru and was inspired by its many underground passageways. Constructing tunnels to the Japanese embassy became the key to freeing the hostages.

The National Intelligence Service was put in charge of the tunnel-building. To provide the labor, professional miners were brought to Lima from their jobs in the Andes Mountains. Their mission was to construct a network of rescue tunnels as quickly and as silently as possible.

There were to be five tunnels—one main and four branches—about 3 m (10 ft.) below ground. They would be braced with steel and large enough to allow commandos to move upright and in pairs. The main tunnel, at least, would be air-conditioned, equipped with electric lights and communication lines, and padded with heavy carpet to dampen sounds. It would be stocked with weapons and food.

Teams of miners worked around the clock in four-hour shifts for several weeks. They built tunnels from houses in the embassy neighborhood to main points under the mansion's grounds, such as the area where the rebels played soccer, the kitchen, and the party tent in the garden.

Get Ready...

While the tunnels were being constructed, the armed forces were busy smuggling spy equipment into the embassy. Two-way microphones no bigger than matches were tucked inside books, thermos bottles, and clothing sent to the captives. Hostages who were military and police officers hid these microphones around the embassy. Further, one retired navy officer had a small radio receiver that he had managed to keep since he was first taken captive.

In homes on the streets surrounding the mansion, intelligence officers used high-tech equipment to talk with the hostages and to eavesdrop on the rebels. The information they discovered was critical to the success of Operation Chavin de Huantar. The officers learned how the rebels organized their days, what weapons they had, and when they most expected to be attacked (at night). They also found out where the hostages were kept and when and where the rebels played soccer each afternoon. Cerpa had unknowingly made a rescue attempt easier by herding all the hostages onto the same floor and by playing soccer at roughly the same time each day.

Meanwhile, 140 of Peru's finest commandos from the army, navy, and air force were sent to a port city near Lima. There, a rough replica of the embassy had been built for training purposes. The commandos experimented with various tactics for bursting in on the rebels and taking control of the embassy. They tested out the use of different types of explosives and weapons. And they practiced their moves over and over.

The commandos knew that timing was critical to saving lives inside the embassy. By their calculations, they would need just six minutes to rescue the hostages and another twenty minutes to make sure the building was clearly out of enemy hands.

Get Set...

Tuesday, April 22, 1997. "There it is again," thought the Bolivian ambassador, "the anthem of the Peruvian navy." THRUM-DA-DA-DA-DUM. Shivers raced up his spine as he listened to the music pouring from loudspeakers on the embassy grounds. He had heard it playing yesterday, too, and he recognized it for what it was: a signal. Hear the anthem on two consecutive days and expect a rescue attempt before nightfall. Operation Chavin de Huantar was about to come to a head.

The previous day, many of the specially trained commandos had entered the neighboring houses containing entrances to the tunnels the miners had built. By wearing the uniforms of the police force that had been standing guard around the embassy, the commandos escaped the rebels' attention. Further, they arrived in small groups to avoid attracting any particular notice.

Once inside the tunnels, the troops changed into their camouflage fatigues. Then they spent the long night waiting.

The next morning, the commandos donned their hard helmets and bulletproof vests, and checked over the gas masks, weapons, and explosives they would use. They were soon joined by officers who had held a final planning session. And they all waited some more.

Above ground, intelligence officers were spying on the Tupac Amaru. Using the microphones planted inside the embassy, they were listening in on the rebels and trying to track their movements. The officers hoped that nothing would happen to cause a change in the rebels' routine that day. If everything went as expected, the hostages would all be in their second-floor bedrooms by midafternoon, and most of the rebels would be enjoying a soccer game on the main floor.

Just after 3:00 p.m., one of the hostages whispered a report to the intelligence officers: 8 of the rebels—including Cerpa and his three lieutenants—were playing soccer, another 3 were watching the game from the second floor, a 12th rebel was guarding the front door, a 13th was sitting under the staircase, and the 14th was monitoring the hallway to the hostages' bedrooms. All rebels accounted for!

Go!!

The intelligence officers notified President Fujimori at once. His response was urgent: "GO!" And at that, they contacted the retired naval officer held inside the embassy. They had two requests: prepare the others for an immediate attack, and try to open the metal door to the balcony outside one of the back bedrooms.

Calmly, the retired naval officer spread the message. A few of the hostages struggled with the metal door and managed to open it, but they were faced with a second, wooden door that was bolted shut.

Leaving it, they joined the other hostages and lay down on the floor, covering their faces. If the rebels were looking to kill any one particular hostage, they'd have a much harder time finding the right person. Further, someone flipped the end of a mattress over the head of the Japanese ambassador.

About 3:15 p.m., the soccer-playing rebels had just hollered, "Goal!" when the floor beneath them erupted. Commandos poured into the room from the tunnel below, firing their weapons as they came (see diagram). Their explosives had blown a large hole in the floor, killing some of the rebels instantly. The others leapt for their guns, returning the commandos' fire and racing for the staircase. Cerpa was among them.

At the same time, commandos set off charges from other tunnels, blasting their way into the garden and through the back of the mansion. More commandos raced to the front of the house and blasted their way through the door. Tear gas poured through the windows. Thick smoke filled the embassy. And everywhere, there was a flurry of bullets.

Upstairs, the rebels fired their weapons, mostly shooting back at the commandos. One of the younger members of the MRTA aimed his rifle at a hostage, then lowered it and left the room without firing. Seconds later, he was shot down.

Meanwhile, a team of commandos blew out the bolted wooden door to the balcony off the bedroom. From there, they began leading the badly shaken hostages down an outside stairway to safety.

In the End

It took the commandos a bit longer than they had expected to defeat the Tupac Amaru rebels, move out the hostages, and secure the embassy. Still, newscasts around the world hailed

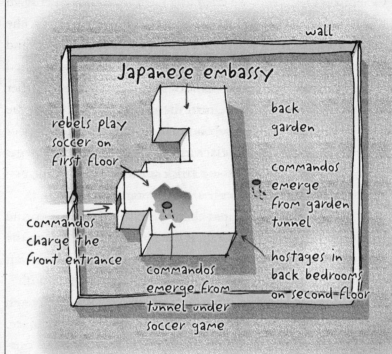

All tunnels were built from neighboring properties.
The final number and locations have not been confirmed.

Operation Chavin de Huantar as one of the most stunning hostage rescues in years. They applauded the speed and efficiency of the raid. They praised its planners for their skill and patience in gathering intelligence, developing strategies, constructing tunnels, and training commandos.

Amazingly, 71 of the 72 hostages who were held captive to the bitter end survived the crisis. The rebels wounded a Peruvian supreme court judge, and he died from a heart attack on his way to the hospital.

The commandos suffered two deaths. One man was killed while opening the balcony door to reach the hostages. Another was gunned down as he helped one of the captives escape.

All 14 of the MRTA rebels, including their leader, Nestor Cerpa, were killed in the attack. Although arguments still rage, reports are that some of the rebels may have tried to surrender but were shot dead on the spot, along with the others.

As the flag of the Tupac Amaru was removed from the embassy, President Fujimori arrived. He joined the commandos and some of the former captives in singing the Peruvian national anthem. The liberated hostages hugged one another in joy and relief. Their long ordeal, which had lasted 126 days, was finally over.

The priest who had insisted on staying with the other captives throughout the crisis tried to describe the commando attack that set them free. "All that you see on television was nothing to the noise, the explosions, and the shocks that we went through," he said. "I was convinced these were the last few minutes of my life." Thanks to Operation Chavin de Huantar, they weren't.

"I think you're just in bed for a rest," teased the prince. "You don't look sick to me." His Royal Highness moved on through the hospital ward, stopping at each bed to shake hands...share a smile...offer a word or two of encouragement. For one patient, he autographed a cast on a broken leg, simply scrawling "Philip." "Don't worry," he murmured. "You'll be out of here before long."

Royalty rarely comes to Springhill, Nova Scotia, a small Canadian town set close to the New Brunswick border. Yet in the fall of 1958, Prince Philip, Duke of Edinburgh, made a point of rescheduling his flight from Ottawa, Ontario, to London, England, so he could make a special visit. Springhill had just weathered one of the worst in a long series of disasters that had killed hundreds of coal miners since the late 1800s. Touched by the tragedy and by the courage of the survivors, the prince had come to pay his respects.

The Bump!

Thursday, October 23, 1958, began as an ordinary day at Springhill's #2 mine. Run by the Cumberland Railway and Coal Company—a branch of the Dominion Steel and Coal Corporation—the coal mine was the deepest in North

America. From the entrance 150 m (490 ft.) above sea level, it sloped steeply for approximately 4,360 m (14,300 ft.). At its lowest point, the mine reached 1,340 m (4,400 ft.) straight down from the surface.

Around 7:00 p.m., miners working the evening shift felt a mild "bump," their word for a sudden shifting of rock underground. It didn't cause much concern. Mining changes the pressure on coal seams and on the layers beneath them, so such bumps are quite common. They're especially frequent in tunnels that are deep underground.

An hour later, shortly after 8:00 p.m., the miners felt a second bump. This one was much, much stronger! Homes in Springhill quivered. Dishes rattled.

But that was nothing compared to what coal miners experienced beneath the surface. The bump was the strongest they had ever felt, and it had caught 174 men working in the tunnels. The force tossed many of them right into the air. Some were crushed beneath crumbling rock and falling mine timbers. Said one, "I was thrown back and hooked underneath the conveyor pan. The coal buried me, except my head, and cut my face pretty bad. I could hear men above me shouting and moaning."

To the Rescue

The quaking ground immediately spurred off-duty miners to action. At home, mine manager George Calder leapt into his car and sped to the pit at once. Officials there told him that the main slope and west walls seemed to be fine, but that the east walls, especially at the deepest levels, were in a shambles. "A pile of spaghetti" was how one miner later described the heaps of posts, rails, and rock. What's more, the bump had released deadly gases from underground pockets, and some were seeping into the tunnels.

In less than 25 minutes, Calder had a rescue operation underway. He personally led a group of 13 workmen and mine officials below to check out the extent of the disaster. Before 9:30 p.m., a crew of volunteer draegermen had moved into the pit. They were miners who were trained to handle underground disasters using specially designed oxygen equipment in gas-filled tunnels.

As more rescue crews arrived, they began working in shifts around the clock, struggling to save the living—and retrieve the dead—from the mine. The pressure was on. The men knew how important it was to reach injured miners as quickly as possible. Still, they had to dig gingerly through the rock piles so they didn't trigger any further slides. Their own lives were constantly in danger.

Meanwhile, navy helicopters from the nearby city of Halifax flew in blood supplies for the injured. Red Cross trucks arrived with beds, and planes loaded with other emergency goods stood by.

A few shaken survivors managed to make their own way out of the mine. Others were hauled out on stretchers, often unconscious. Bill Stevenson, a mine worker for 45 years, was one of the first to be found the day the bump occurred. Despite chest injuries plus a broken leg and shoulder, he had managed to crawl 100 m (330 ft.) along a steep slope in total darkness. Rescuers helped him the rest of the way.

By October 25, 81 of the 174 miners had reached safety.

Rescue crews kept digging...and listening...digging...and hoping. But when Wednesday, October 29, rolled around, they felt forced to accept that the rest of the miners had perished. Disheartened and exhausted, the draegermen continued to work through the wreckage, but they had to dig slowly...carefully. In places, they were able to move less than 0.3 m (1 ft.) of rubble an hour.

The crowds of hopeful family members that waited anxiously at the surface began to thin. Making burial arrangements seemed to be the only thing left for them to do.

The Cage

Inside a tunnel about 4,000 m (13,000 ft.) from the mine's entrance, 12 miners huddled helplessly together (see diagram). On October 23, they had been working in a passage 3 m (10 ft.) high when the ground beneath their feet heaved upward with a roar. Suddenly, they found themselves in a debris-filled "cage" no higher than 1.2 m (4 ft.) and walled in by fallen rock on all sides.

Most of their battery-run lamps had been knocked out in the upheaval, so the men could not even see who lay beside them. Some were coughing, choking on clouds of dust; others were groaning in pain.

Groping their way in the darkness, they crept together to discuss their dilemma. Three of the men had experienced a similar disaster just two years earlier, when another bump had killed 39 miners in the mine next to #2. The trio had been buried for three days. At least, they had learned how to hang onto hope.

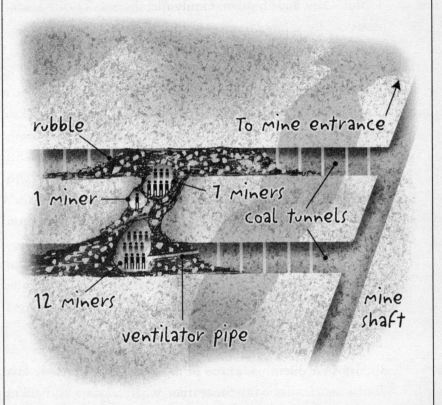

rubble

To mine entrance

1 miner

7 miners

coal tunnels

12 miners

ventilator pipe

mine shaft

By feeling around, they discovered an opening at one end of their cage. The men formed a human chain and held onto one another while the front man crawled through. But he quickly detected a pocket of strong gas and retreated at once. There was no escape. They were trapped.

Refusing to give in to despair, the miners focused on finding supplies that might help them survive until they were found. They had to move cautiously, though. They couldn't risk disturbing any more loose rock.

The treasures they managed to gather included a lamp that still worked, half a can of water, and a few sandwiches left in lunch pails after the supper break. One of the miners had a watch with a luminous dial. At least, they could keep track of the time they had left.

To help boost their spirits, the miners told every joke they could remember. Two of them were choir members, and they sang a few songs. What the men didn't do was talk of their families or friends. They weren't sure they'd ever see their loved ones again, and those thoughts were best kept private.

On the third day, one of the miners recalled that someone had hung a carrot on the wall to tease a fellow nicknamed "Rabbit." Feeling his way along, he managed to find it and added it to the group's meager stock of food. Never had a carrot meant so much.

By October 27, supplies were running dangerously low. The miners rationed their last few drops of water, half-filling a small Aspirin bottle and passing it around.

For one or two days, the miners thought they heard clinking and tapping—sounds of rescuers digging nearby. They had tried shouting, but their only reply was an eerie echo. They had also taken turns striking a ventilator pipe that was sticking through the rock. But there had been no response.

Another 24 hours passed, and the miners grew weaker. Their thirst was overwhelming. Their lips were cracked and swollen. Falling into a dreamlike state, they imagined they were seeing bright lights—yellow lights—heading their way.

When October 29 arrived, the water was gone. The miners were forced to drink their own urine. Even the supply of fresh air that reached their cage seemed to dwindle. They knew they couldn't hold on much longer.

Springhill Miracle

Then they heard it: clunk, clunk. Something was definitely hitting the far end of the ventilator pipe. As weak as they were, two of the miners called up from their cage, and back came a faint "Hello."

Work crews checking for bodies had discovered the broken end of the ventilator pipe sticking out of the rubble. They had sent for someone to test the pipe for gas, and as he was checking it, he thought he heard voices. At the sound of his "Hello," the voices grew stronger. One hollered, "There are 12 of us in here. Come and get us."

This "Springhill Miracle," as reporters around the world called it, occurred near 2:30 p.m. on October 29. The news that there were still survivors in the mine spurred the flagging rescue efforts and drew the townspeople back to the pit. Hope was in the air once more.

Still, the crews couldn't reach the trapped miners quickly.

The barrier of rock and rubble was still about 22 m (72 ft.) thick, and despite their excitement, the rescuers had to dig gently.

To keep the survivors alive, they tried passing a rubber hose through the steel pipe so they could pour in liquids. It jammed, but they quickly sent up for a narrow copper tube, which they were able to shove through the pipe. Then they pumped in life-saving water, sugared coffee, and soup to the men. The mine's doctor was on hand, warning the starving miners not to drink the liquids too fast—something that could make them sick, as their bodies could no longer process normal portions.

It was 2:30 a.m. the next day before rescuers reached the miners—12 hours after first discovering their "cage." It took another two hours to carry the men up to the surface.

Trembling on their stretchers, the miners turned tear-stained, blackened faces toward the cheering crowd of well-wishers and reporters. One injured man managed to prop himself up and wave. Considering his six-and-a-half-day ordeal, he commented sadly, "I think we must be the only ones left alive." But he was wrong...

Seven More!

Amazingly, two days later—at 4:00 a.m., November 1—rescuers discovered another seven survivors trapped in a pocket just a bit higher up than where the other 12 had been found.

One of those seven, miner Garnet Clarke, reported hearing a loud thud the day the bump knocked him to the ground. The next thing he knew he was imprisoned in a rock cell with six others. About 30 m (100 ft.) away, a much smaller hole held another miner captive. The group could hear him, but there was no way they could reach him.

Their battery-powered lamps didn't last long. As the light in the tunnel grew dim, the miners wrote their names on a rough timber. They figured it would help rescuers identify their bodies if help arrived too late. Then they were plunged into total darkness.

The men pooled the food they had: about 1 l (1 qt.) of water, a little tea, a few sandwiches, and a bit of cake. As day followed day, they had to supplement their skimpy diet by chewing moist bark off mine timbers, sucking lumps of coal, and drinking their own urine.

October 27 was Clarke's 29th birthday. Being buried deep underground was no way to celebrate, but the men did what they could. They ate a few scraps from their precious food supply and sang "Happy Birthday." It's not hard to guess what Clarke's birthday wish must have been.

The miners struggled to keep their minds active and their spirits up. They chatted, joked, and sang together in the dark. But no one joked and sang more than Maurice Ruddick. For years, he had entertained the folks of Springhill with his rich baritone voice. But in that pit, he sang as if life depended on it. It very nearly did.

"Maurice Ruddick is the one that kept our hopes alive," a miner later told reporters—and hopes were all they had left.

Early on Saturday, November 1, the draegermen heard noises coming from behind a wall of jumbled rock. Scarcely daring to believe they might find life, they dug nonstop for three hours, working their way carefully through about 4 m (13 ft.) of loose debris.

Inside their cell, the miners were so weak they weren't even aware that rescuers were near. When the crews broke through the wall, they found Ruddick still singing. Now he really had something to sing about.

Frail and worn from eight and a half days underground, the men finally reached the surface at 9:15 a.m. The rescuers had freed the solitary miner from his lonely cell nearby and saved six of the seven who had been imprisoned together.

By November 6, all 174 of the miners had been found; 100 of them were still alive. Sadly, Bill Stevenson, one of the first men rescued the day of the bump, died from his injuries later in the month. That raised the final death toll to 75. And the whole tragedy brought an end to major coal mining in Springhill, Nova Scotia. It was the last straw.

Postscript

Like millions of other people around the world, the governor of the state of Georgia had tuned in to the news as the drama at Springhill unfolded. The courage of the miners who had been trapped underground impressed him so much that he invited them to be guests at a luxury resort. Those who were able to travel were thrilled.

Then the governor discovered that Maurice Ruddick was Black. At the time, southern states such as Georgia had racist laws preventing Black people from mixing with Whites. The governor changed his invitation, telling Ruddick that he could still come to Georgia, but he wouldn't be able to stay at the resort with the other miners.

The Springhill men refused to go without him. As one of them put it, "There was no segregation down that hole, and there's none in this group." They knew how important Ruddick had been in raising their spirits. But Ruddick wanted the survivors to enjoy their heroes' holiday, so he accepted the restricted invitation and went to Georgia to be honored by its Black community.

Many years later, Canadian folk singer Val MacDonald paid a special tribute to Maurice Ruddick—her father. She recorded a song that he had written, one that he had begun to compose while he was still trapped underground: "The Springhill Mine Disaster Song."

"Hang in," he thought, "don't lose your cool. It's pitch-black in this tunnel, so crawl s-l-o-w-l-y. That's it. Bit by bit, feel your way: the floor beneath your belly...the walls by your sides...the ceiling right above your head. Tune your body to the tunnel and you just might stay alive."

Beads of sweat formed on the soldier's brow. His breathing was rapid as he struggled to hold back the panic that was welling up inside. This was nothing like fighting on the surface...in the air...in the light...in all that space. Deep in the coffinlike tunnel, the world pressed in around him. No choice but to twist and turn with its dips and bends, and to squeeze through more trapdoors along the way.

"Yeow! Fire ants!" he screamed silently. He'd taped the tops of his boots to his pants, but the ants got in anyway. Nothing to do but let them bite and endure their painful, burning stings. Pinned inside the tunnel, he couldn't reach his feet if he tried. Nor could he rub them against the tunnel floor. He dared not make a sound. Just ahead might be the enemy, crouched and ready to slit his throat.

Cautiously, the soldier continued to slide his hands across the tunnel surfaces. His left thumb touched something smooth and hard—there, on the ceiling. Bamboo, he figured. Bump against it and he might disturb a venomous snake. Sometimes, the enemy tied a viper inside a length of hollow bamboo, just waiting for a passing soldier to knock it out. Best to stay low and wriggle on. If he tried to shoot the snake, he'd reveal his location.

Welcome to Vietnam

The soldier was an American fighting a strange battle far from home. Between 1965 and 1972, ground troops from the United States joined South Vietnam in a war against the official armed forces of North Vietnam and a guerrilla force, called the Vietcong. Like guerrillas anywhere, the Vietcong were soldiers, mostly volunteers, who made surprise attacks behind enemy lines. Working mainly from a network of underground tunnels in the Cu Chi district of South Vietnam, the Vietcong made a formidable army.

The Cu Chi district was an area of villages, rice paddies, orchards, and plantations. It sat close to the South Vietnamese capital of Saigon (now called Ho Chi Minh City). The district was an ideal place for the Vietcong to conduct warfare—to collect supplies, assemble troops, and make attacks.

Cu Chi was also perfect for tunneling. Its reddish soil was mostly hard iron clay—sticky and stable—and the water table was usually 10 to 20 m (33 to 66 ft.) down. Although digging through dry clay was tough work for the Vietcong, the results were impressive. Tunnel walls and ceilings held like concrete. Even exploding grenades did little more than make a few holes or cracks. The passageways themselves failed to collapse.

Back in the 1940s, the Vietnamese had already created the basic tunnel system. At the time, Vietnam—North and South as one country—was fighting for independence from France. Families had dug simple underground shelters as hiding places and linked them with their neighbors' shelters or with those in other villages. Vietnam won the war in 1954, but was divided into two nations: Communist North Vietnam and anti-Communist South Vietnam.

When the Vietcong went to war against the South Vietnamese and the Americans in the 1960s, the guerrillas adopted the existing tunnel network and expanded it—particularly in Cu Chi (see diagram). This underground base was their best defence against an enemy who was much more powerfully armed. And it turned out to be especially well placed when American forces unwittingly built a large military camp right above the Cu Chi tunnels!

The Burrowers

Hundreds of kilometers of passageways made up the expanded underground network, which formed as many as four levels in places. Building all these tunnels required the labor of almost everybody—men, women, boys, and girls—who supported and fought for the Vietcong. They dug most passages with the simple spades and hoes that peasants used every day in the fields. Some diggers were able to work faster than others, but on average, each person scooped out a pile of dirt the size of a stove per day.

Together, they removed thousands of tons of soil, which they had to dump well away from the tunnels—without attracting the eye of the enemy. Bit by bit, they hauled it all away, often in small, homemade baskets or in containers of food.

Section of Vietcong Tunnels in Cu Chi District

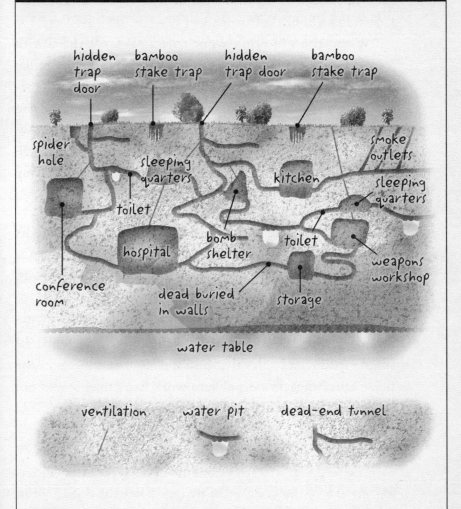

hidden trap door

bamboo stake trap

hidden trap door

bamboo stake trap

spider hole

sleeping quarters

kitchen

smoke outlets

sleeping quarters

toilet

hospital

bomb shelter

toilet

weapons workshop

conference room

dead buried in walls

storage

water table

ventilation

water pit

dead-end tunnel

Then they secretly hid the soil, by digging it into the earth on farms, sprinkling it in fast-moving streams, adding it to building foundations, and depositing it in holes made by bombs.

Over the topmost level of the tunnels, the diggers left a depth of soil about as thick and as protective as 10 mattresses. Where the tunnels widened to form large open rooms, roofs were reinforced with layers of bamboo poles and coconut husks.

Gateways to the Underground

The Vietcong planned and built their tunnel entrances well. Each group of burrows normally had three gateways, arranged like points in a triangle and set quite a distance apart. If one entrance was blocked or destroyed, the others would allow the guerrillas to get in—or out.

All entrances were set in well-drained spots that wouldn't be easily flooded. They were closed over with wooden trapdoors with edges that were beveled—cut at an angle—for strength. The doors could stand up to heavy pressure without sagging or sinking.

For security, all trapdoors were made as invisible as possible by blending them with their surroundings. The Vietcong covered some with soil and living plants, and smothered others with layers of dead leaves, often collected by children. Entrances close to houses or farms were built wherever the enemy wasn't likely to check—such as beneath stinky manure piles inside pig pens.

Small holes in the trapdoors let in air and light. The openings were drilled at angles. Some were slanted to catch the light; others, to catch the wind. Rain that fell through the holes drained into hollows dug along the sloping floors inside the passageways.

Life in the Dirt

Imagine how harsh life would have been in the Cu Chi tunnels. They were hot, dark, and ridden with insects, rodents, and snakes. Yet the Vietcong lived in them for years, laboring hard for their cause. They made weapons from unexploded enemy shells, pedaled bicycles to produce electricity, and even cared for sick and wounded soldiers—all underground.

Tunnel doctors struggled to save lives under the most primitive conditions. They draped the dirt walls of their "hospitals" with abandoned American parachutes, reducing the risk of infection. They used rough tools made of metal scavenged from fallen enemy aircraft. And if there wasn't enough electricity to produce light, they slapped on miners' hats with battery-run lamps and kept on working.

During life-threatening enemy attacks, the Vietcong scurried into small bomb shelters within the tunnels. The teepee-like shape of these shelters reduced the shocks from the bombings and also amplified the noise from approaching planes—providing warnings, of sorts.

Exhausted by nightfall, many tunnel workers had to sleep in spaces only the size of playpens. Others shared rooms just big enough for a pair of hammocks. As little air flowed through their quarters, the smell of sweat and excrement was sickening. Tunnel "toilets" were simply holes or large jars set in the floor. When full, they were covered over with dirt, but the stench lingered on.

Regular food supplies—usually rice—were meager, but sometimes they were supplemented with grilled rats or with tinned meat and other supplies left behind at American army camps. The meals were cooked in crowded kitchens. Smoke from each stove was channeled out through several different exits so it would not be noticed and reveal the location of a tunnel system. Still, the ducts often leaked smoke into the passageways, making it hard for tunnel dwellers to breathe.

The Vietcong also had to share the tunnels with the dead. While battles raged, it wasn't safe to bury anyone at the surface, so the Vietcong set up sections of the passageways as temporary cemeteries. They placed the bodies, curled up, in shallow "graves" inside walls.

Through the Maze

The underground tunnels were not easy to navigate. Some were so narrow a person couldn't turn around in them. Many sets of tunnels included secret corridors, used for making surprise attacks. There were even dead-end passages to confuse invaders.

Few of the passages ran in straight lines for any distance, but that helped protect the Vietcong. By zigzagging sharply—and sloping up and down—the passages made it hard for enemies to fire at the guerrillas or toss explosives any distance.

As well, the corridors passed through deep, U-shaped pits, dug to gather water. The pits kept chemical weapons such as tear gas from traveling the length of a passageway. Swimming across these pits was the only way to get past them.

Sealed trapdoors with air holes connected the different

levels of passages. Just like the doors at tunnel entrances, these were well hidden. If enemy soldiers discovered one level of a tunnel system, they wouldn't necessarily discover another. Even if they did find the doors, enemy soldiers may not have been able to figure out how to open them. Only the Vietcong soldiers knew to feel in the dirt for the wires that unfastened the doors.

Controlling Cu Chi

So cleverly were the tunnels designed that the Vietcong managed to control the Cu Chi district for years. Peering out from their underground base, they kept a close watch on American troops. That helped them plan attacks and choose locations for traps.

The Vietcong struck mostly at night, rising from their underworld to wound and kill soldiers with grenades and rifles. During the day, snipers fired at the enemy from one-person "spider holes." The shoulder-deep dugouts were well camouflaged and set near tunnel entrances. After taking their shots, the snipers disappeared through short tunnels that connected the spider holes to main tunnels.

Sometimes, the Vietcong planted surprises. They would bury a land mine near a tunnel entrance, then deliberately exposed the location of the entrance. When enemy soldiers found it, they gathered around to support whoever volunteered to explore the tunnel. Then the Vietcong would explode the land mine.

At other times, the guerrillas would remove the safety pin from a grenade and hide it by a tunnel. When the enemy came near, they pulled a thin wire attached to the grenade and...BLAST!

Explosions weren't even the most gruesome method the Vietcong used to defend their tunnels. Around entrances, they frequently dug open pits and covered them with layers of branches. At the bottoms of the pits, they stuck in sharp bamboo stakes that speared soldiers who fell in.

The American Response

Even if American troops searched an area thoroughly by sticking knives and bayonets in the ground, they had a hard time finding tunnel entrances. Unlike the Vietcong, who knew their enemy's ways well, the U.S. soldiers had a lot to learn about the tunnelers and their techniques. But when the Americans realized that the Vietcong were scavenging goods, they set traps to locate some of the tunnels. They bugged radios that "accidentally" fell from their aircraft, then followed the electronic signals as the guerrillas took the radios to their tunnels.

Even harder than finding the tunnels was figuring out how to destroy them or to kill the guerrillas inside. The underground passages were so well designed that pumping in smoke, gases, or water had little effect. Explosives tossed into the tunnels did no real damage.

Sending regular American soldiers underground to fight the Vietcong was not the answer, either. Few had ever come across anything like these mazes, and most were too big to fit through them. Those who could get in often failed to survive. The Vietcong were waiting with hidden traps and explosives. Here and there, a guerrilla crouched behind a false wall made of a thin layer of clay and kept watch through a spy hole. As an enemy crept through a tunnel, the guerrilla attacked through the wall with a bamboo spear.

But among the American forces were a few soldiers who were especially well suited to explore the tunnels of Vietnam. They were small enough to travel the narrow passageways, and they didn't tend to panic in dark, enclosed places. They received special training that prepared them for challenges such as hand-to-hand combat inside the Cu Chi tunnels.

Unlike other American soldiers, these underground warriors—called Tunnel Rats—worked with a minimum of equipment. They preferred the freedom of moving unburdened through the tunnels. A knife was what they valued most. With a sharp blade, they could probe the ground to feel for trapdoors and attack an enemy in silence. For backup, they also packed a pistol and a small flashlight.

To survive, the Tunnel Rats depended less on sight and more on their other senses. In the darkness of the underground, they learned to do a great deal by touch alone—everything from changing the tiny bulb in a flashlight to feeling for booby traps in tunnel walls. They sniffed the stale air for any scent of a living body. And they listened carefully for the sound of danger: the rustling of clothes or the faint breathing of a nearby enemy.

When they emerged from the tunnels, the Rats usually made a point of flashing red lights or whistling an American tune. It was their way of announcing who they were so their own troops wouldn't accidentally shoot them.

The Bomb

The Tunnel Rats had their victories, catching and killing the enemy, but it was the bomb that finally defeated the Vietcong. The underground fortress of Cu Chi crumbled under attacks from B-52 bombers—big, high-altitude planes that carried more than 100 bombs each. The strikes were so powerful they could be felt 32 km (20 mi.) away. Buildings, trees, rock, and people were blown to bits. Some of the bombs plunged meters underground before exploding. They created deep pits and damaged tunnels so heavily that they were no longer usable. Nor could they be repaired.

The decision to use bombs in the Cu Chi district—within South Vietnam—however, came too late to defeat North Vietnam. Fighting from their tunnels, the Vietcong guerrillas had managed to drag out the war long enough to cripple their enemies. In 1972, the last of the American ground forces left for home.

War between the North and South continued until 1975, when South Vietnam was defeated. The following year, the two countries officially reunited.

Howard Carter stood at the far end of a dark tunnel 7 m (23 ft.) beneath a valley floor in Egypt. In front of him was an opening that had been sealed shut with gray plaster and stamped with symbols of ancient royalty. Trembling in anticipation, he hammered out a small hole in an upper corner of the plaster. Next, he lit a candle and stuck it through the hole to test for foul gases. The flame flickered in the stale air, then burned steadily.

Carter widened the opening and inserted the candle once more—this time, to provide some light. He peered anxiously through the hole. Only two or three minutes passed, but his friends could barely stand the wait.

"Can you see anything?" gasped one of them.

"Yes...WONDERFUL things!" Carter replied. Without another word, he widened the hole for the others to peek through and switched on a flashlight.

Strange shadows played on the walls inside. Carved beasts—cheetahs, hippopotamuses, and cows—all with long, slender bodies, formed the sides of large, couchlike beds. Two life-sized statues of black kings in gold kilts and sandals stood on guard, each holding a staff and a mace. And all around the room sat vases, chairs, boxes, and bouquets of dried leaves. There was even a golden throne, and in one corner, some overturned chariots.

The day was November 26, 1922. "The day of days," Carter later wrote of his experience, "the most wonderful that I have ever lived through, and certainly one whose like I can never hope to see again." For Carter had discovered the richest tomb in all of Egypt: the final resting place of King Tutankhamun— lost for more than 3,000 years!

Child-King

Tutankhamun, or Tut, as he's often called today, was only seven or eight years old when he mounted the throne to rule Egypt circa 1333 BC. He became a god-king, or pharaoh—a negotiator between divine beings and human beings.

Not only was Tut extremely young for the job, he came to power during very troubled times. Apart from the brief rule of a temporary pharaoh, named Smenkhkare, Tut followed the much hated King Akhenaten to the throne. During a 17-year reign, Akhenaten had tried to force Egyptians to worship a single god, instead of all the many ones they believed in. He had ordered statues of these other gods destroyed or disfigured, and their names removed from wherever they had been carved or written.

Not surprisingly, when young Tut took the throne, there were many advisors wanting to tell him what to do. Chief among them was his forceful stepgrandfather, Ay. Tut listened to his advisors well and returned Egypt to the worship of many gods.

But Ay longed to run Egypt himself, and that desire may

have driven him to commit murder. Twentieth-century X-rays of the body of King Tut show that he might have died at age 17 or 18 from heavy blows to his head. Ay became the next king, ruling for four years.

A military leader, named General Horemheb, took over Egypt after Ay's rule. He hadn't been happy with the four previous kings, so he wiped the records clean of Ay, Tut, Smenkhkare, and Akhenaten. It was as if they had never existed, and over time, Egypt forgot them.

Tut's Burial

Like other royalty and privileged people of the day, Tut had been buried in the Valley of the Kings. It was a barren site on the west bank of the River Nile. By placing the bodies and their possessions in this isolated cemetery, the Egyptians had tried to prevent grave robberies. A narrow gorge was the only entrance to the valley, and armed sentries guarded it day and night.

Tut's body had been preserved and buried with everything Egyptians thought the king might need to live well in an afterlife: food, clothing, furniture, chariots, and many treasures. To do less—even for a low-ranking king such as Tut—could cause trouble. The Egyptians believed that if a pharaoh wasn't well equipped for his journeys after death, the sun might stop shining, and the moon might never be seen again. The world would plunge into chaos.

Most pharaohs spent years planning and supervising the building of large, elaborate tombs for themselves, but young Tut barely had a chance to begin his. Instead, the child-king's final resting place was small and plain. It was likely a tomb intended for someone else—certainly not a pharaoh—then quickly adapted for his use. Stonecutters had tunneled it out of rock in a low-lying part of the valley floor. Over time, desert winds and storms buried the tomb completely, blending the grave site with its surroundings.

So hidden and forgotten was the tomb that, two centuries later, King Ramses VI had his own tomb built within several steps of it. Unknowingly, his workers put their huts right on top of the entrance to Tut's tomb, hiding it even more.

Another 60 years passed, and the tomb was overlooked again when King Ramses XI began to dismantle the royal cemetery. Sentries had been unable to protect it from a steady assault by thieves, so the bodies of many of the pharaohs were moved to secret burial sites that were easier to guard.

Foxes, desert owls, and colonies of bats moved into the empty tombs in the deserted Valley of the Kings. But through it all, Tut remained in his original grave. His disappearance from history records at the hand of General Horemheb and his burial in a simple tomb made it possible for him to rest in peace for more than 30 centuries.

The Buccaneers

Along came two British adventurers, Howard Carter and Lord George Herbert Carnarvon, who met in 1907. Neither of them had had any formal education in Egyptian history or archeology. Carnarvon had begun exploring Egypt's tomb sites as a hobby after injuries from a car accident in Germany forced him to spend winters in a warm country. He hired work crews to dig for ancient treasures, at first finding nothing more than a mummified cat in a cat-shaped coffin. To ancient Egyptians, cats were sacred animals.

Howard Carter's talents as an artist had taken him to Egypt at age 17 to help reproduce drawings found on walls in ancient temples and tombs. Once there, he got the chance to join digging teams. By the time he met Carnarvon, he'd had years of experience tunneling in Egypt's tomb sites. Carnarvon hired Carter as a field director for his own explorations.

The two became close friends, eventually sharing 16 years of adventures in Egypt. They commonly marked their exploration sites with two back-to-back, interlinked Cs, which roughly resembled the skull and crossbones on the flags of pirates—or buccaneers. The symbol earned Carter and Carnarvon the nickname "Buccaneers."

By 1917, the Buccaneers focused their efforts on finding King Tut's tomb. The existence of a pharaoh named Tut had come to light in the Valley of the Kings with the discovery of a few objects that bore his name. One was a glazed clay cup, discovered under a rock in 1905. Tomb robbers may have mistaken it for glass—highly valued in ancient times—then dumped it when they realized what they'd actually stolen. Not far from the cup lay a broken wooden box containing bits of gold foil that revealed the names of King Tutankhamun and his queen.

The Buccaneers began searching for the tomb of the mystery pharaoh. Bit by bit, they worked their way across the floor of the Valley of the Kings, clearing away soil, rock, and stone right down to bedrock. Workers carted away thousands of tons of material. The costs were enormous.

One More Look

By 1922, Lord Carnarvon was ready to give up. The search for King Tut had been very expensive, yet it had uncovered no clues leading to his tomb. Carnarvon, who had returned to England, tried to call off the exploration. But Carter met with him and offered to check just one more part of the Valley, at his own expense. Carnarvon was so impressed with Carter's determination that he agreed to the proposal—and he funded it, too.

Back in the Valley of the Kings, Carter set to work on November 1, 1922, close to the tomb of Ramses VI. His crew hauled away the remains of several huts once used by the builders of that tomb. Then they started to clear away the soil that lay a meter (3 ft.) deep beneath the huts. As workers dug where the first hut had stood, they came to a sudden stop. To their great surprise, they'd unearthed a step that was cut into rock.

Over the next day and a half, the crew worked furiously, exposing all four sides of what appeared to be a sunken staircase. Carter knew it had to be the opening to a tomb. But whose?

More steps in the staircase were uncovered. The workers descended into a mostly enclosed stairwell with a high ceiling. By sunset on November 5, when the 12th step had been uncovered, Carter could just make out the upper part of an entranceway sealed with plaster. He cut a small opening in it and found a corridor filled from floor to ceiling with stone and debris.

Stifling an overwhelming desire to tunnel through it, Carter decided to wait for Lord Carnarvon to come from England. Then they would be able to share the thrill of this discovery. Carter closed up the hole he had made and had his workers bury the staircase for safekeeping.

"At last have made wonderful discovery in Valley..." Carter wrote in the telegram that brought Lord Carnarvon rushing back to Egypt with his daughter, Lady Evelyn Herbert. Carter also invited his good friend and engineer, Arthur Callender, to join them.

By November 24, all four explorers were gathered at the site. The entire staircase had been completely dug out. A total of 16 steps and the covered entranceway, now fully exposed, lay before them. On the bottom half of the entranceway, the symbols marked in the plaster were very plain. The name of King Tutankhamun stood out loud and clear!

But the team's excitement was dampened when they noticed that the plaster over the entrance had been broken—not just once, but twice. Both times, the hole had been patched, then stamped again with royal symbols. Robbers must have breached the tomb. The team could only hope that little had been damaged or stolen.

Into the Tomb

As Carter had already noticed through the peephole he'd made earlier, the entranceway led to a corridor stuffed with rubble. The Egyptians had filled the tunnel to discourage robbers from invading it. But Carter could see where robbers had once tunneled through the rubble. Their burrow had been refilled with dark stone, unlike the white limestone chips in the rest of the corridor.

Carter's workers began to clear the passageway, which stood 2 m (7 ft.) tall. And as they did, they found several scattered objects, such as alabaster jars and painted vases. The mess confirmed that robbers had reached the tomb before them.

By November 26, the entire length of the corridor was empty—all 7.5 m (25 ft.) of it—and the team stood before a second closed entrance, similar to the first. The plaster showed it also had been broken, then patched and resealed.

It was through the small hole that Carter made in this plaster that he and his three friends caught their first breathtaking glimpse of the many treasures within: the carved bedsides in the shape of cheetahs, hippos, and cows, the two black kings, the golden throne, the chariots, and more. As Carter said, it was indeed "the day of days!"

At that moment, the team didn't feel that more than 3,000 years separated them from the people who had built this tunnel tomb. It was as if someone had been there earlier that very day. A worker had left behind a half-empty bowl of mortar and a lamp he'd been using. And on one wall, a careless finger had marred the once fresh paint job.

There was no coffin in sight, but Carter and Carnarvon noticed a sealed entranceway between the two statues. They knew it must lead to another room.

Taking Stock

The next day, a crew installed lighting, and the four friends finally entered the room, later called the Antechamber (see diagram). They began recording all the wondrous objects it held. One large, couchlike bed stood in front of another sealed doorway leading from the room. At the bottom of the entrance was a hole that had never been repaired. They wriggled beneath the couch to take a look.

Rays from their flashlights flickered across a room that sat

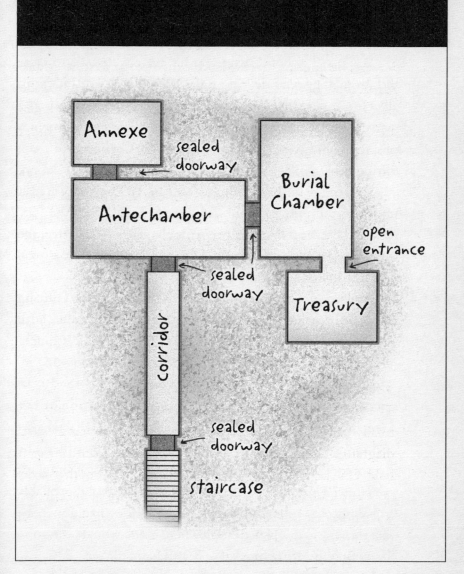

a meter (3 ft.) lower than the Antechamber they were in. This second room was small and crowded. It looked as if robbers had once been there, too. They had ripped through everything in it, dumping out boxes and tossing around silver vessels, feather-filled cushions, and jewelry chests.

Years later, when Carter and his crew were able to clear this room, they recorded more than 2,000 individual items in all! The Annexe, as it was called, had likely been set up as a storage chamber for furniture and perishable goods, such as oils, food, and wine, which a pharaoh was believed to need during his afterlife.

Still, the team hadn't found Tut's body. They expected it might lie through the doorway that was flanked by the statues of the kings, back in the Antechamber. That entrance showed signs of a recovered hole—one no larger than a small person could pass through.

By late November, they decided to break in. Cutting through the patch, Carter squeezed into another room. Lord Carnarvon and Lady Herbert followed him. Callender, unfortunately, was too large and had to be content with looking in.

Like the Annexe, the floor to this small room—the Burial Chamber—lay a meter (3 ft.) beneath the floor of the Antechamber. As soon as the team entered it, they faced a set of floorless golden shrines, stacked one inside the other. The shrines took up most of the room, from wall to wall and floor to ceiling. The outermost shrine was not sealed—probably broken into by robbers, but that's as far as they had gone. The next shrine was unopened. Somewhere inside would lie a coffin containing the King himself—Tutankhamun!

A low, open doorway off the Burial Chamber revealed a fourth and final room, the Treasury. Among the many wonders that filled it was a beautiful shrine that contained four elaborate jars. They held Tut's lungs, liver, stomach, and intestines—organs removed from the body because they were expected to decompose first. There was also a plain wooden box no more than 60 cm (2 ft.) long. Inside lay two tiny coffins, each containing the preserved remains of an unborn child, probably Tut's.

The Pharaoh and his Curse

After the team left the Burial Chamber, they hid the entrance behind a basket and an armful of dry rushes. They planned to hold an official opening later—one that dignitaries and news reporters could attend—and "discover" the shrines.

In February 1923, they did just that, when Carter and Carnarvon announced to the world that King Tut had been found, undisturbed in his tomb. Later, when they opened the shrines, his carefully preserved body was revealed inside a coffin of solid gold.

But all did not go smoothly for the Buccaneers. Lord Carnarvon was shaving one morning when his razor scraped a small mosquito bite on his cheek. The bite became infected. Carnarvon developed pneumonia and died on April 5, 1923. Superstition blamed his death on the fact that he had disturbed the burial site of a pharaoh.

The public and the press went wild searching for misfortunes connected to the exploration of Tut's tomb. As evidence of a "pharaoh's curse," they reported that a cobra had swallowed Carter's canary the day the tomb was opened and that an X-ray specialist had died while traveling to Egypt to examine Tut's body. True, but the same people ignored all those who had been involved with the tomb yet had not been struck by disaster. As Howard Carter told reporters, "I have been finding tombs in ancient Egypt for 34 years, and my health is still good, isn't it?" In fact, he lived to turn 64 in 1939.

Reading the Clues

The job of recording the contents of King Tut's tomb wasn't completed until the spring of 1932, 10 years after Carter and Carnarvon first discovered it. Unlike the heavily raided tombs of most pharaohs, Tut's grave still contained many ornaments and charms as well as the basics: food, clothing, lamps, furniture, chariots, and weapons. Personal treasures—jewelry, musical instruments, and even a lock of his grandmother's hair—were also tucked away with Tut. Along with the drawings in his sparsely decorated tomb, all these objects helped historians learn much about the child-king and life in ancient Egypt.

What was missing from the tomb, such as many of the cosmetic containers that would have been buried with Tut, was also revealing. Fat-based cosmetics, which were popular in his lifetime, were worth stealing, but they didn't last long. Carter figured the tomb must have been robbed within the first 10 to 15 years after Tut died. Also missing were oils, linens, metals, and glass—things that early Egyptians could use or sell easily at the time.

The robbers were likely some of the workers who had helped bury Tut. They knew what was stored with him and exactly where to find it. Repairs to the tomb indicated that the crimes had been detected in ancient times. If the robbers had been caught, they would have been severely punished. They would have had the soles of their feet whipped, and then they would have been executed—tossed onto sharp stakes. In their case, the "curse" on those who dared to enter a pharaoh's tomb would definitely have come true!

"Somebody went to considerable expense to make sure this was a safe entry to go through," an investigator told reporters.

Safe? From prying eyes, maybe. But the "entry" they were discussing was no more than a narrow dirt tunnel 4.5 m (15 ft.) underground. It stood just over a meter (about 4 ft.) high—far too low for adults to walk upright—and it stretched a distance one and a half times the length of a hockey rink. What's more, it ran right under the Mexican-American border. Every step taken through that dim passageway must have been filled with suspense.

In the spring of 1999, 13 people were charged with smuggling cocaine through the tunnel. They had been sneaking shipments underground from Naco, Mexico, to Naco, Arizona, then sending them on to Los Angeles, California. From there, the cocaine was distributed to drug dealers in several American cities and peddled almost everywhere—pool halls, video arcades, nightclubs, restaurants, shopping centers, parking lots, offices, and even schools.

The investigators who searched the tunnel seized 1,200 kg (2,600 lb.) of cocaine and $1.5 million in cash—likely just a chunk of what had already passed through it.

American-Mexican Smuggling Sites

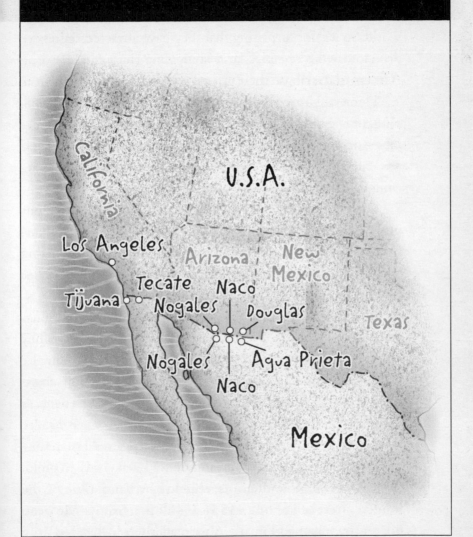

Tapping the Market

Naco, Mexico, and Naco, Arizona, are not the only border towns where mood-altering drugs, such as cocaine and marijuana, are smuggled through tunnels (see map). The American markets for illegal narcotics are some of richest anywhere in the world. So it's not surprising that they have attracted aggressive drug lords who organize large smuggling rings and hire drug runners to distribute their goods.

Desperate poverty can push almost anyone into drug running. In Mexico, many people are unable to find well-paying jobs—or any jobs at all—so they have to struggle to house and feed their families. By comparison, even modestly paid drug runners make big money.

Some of these runners strap or tape narcotics to their bodies, or stuff them into hidden pockets or jacket linings. Others swallow small containers packed with drugs, courting death if any of them crack open. One man even had a surgeon insert packages of cocaine into his thighs!

Sometimes, the runners avoid border checkpoints altogether and enter the United States at remote locations. They might choose to backpack drugs across the desert, traveling by horse or by foot. They might move their loot by raft down streams. Or they might creep through the many tunnels beneath the border.

Since 1990, investigators have uncovered several such tunnels. Some were complex and must have been costly to build. Others were simple dugouts, chiseled by hand. One of the longest stretched about 445 m (1460 ft.), from a Mexican border town named Tijuana. A particularly cold-hearted drug lord named Joaquin Guzman, and known as "El Chapo," had ordered it built. According to some reports, he tried to keep the tunnel a secret by killing his laborers as soon as they had finished working on it. But the passage was never used. Despite all the efforts made to hide it, drug agents discovered the tunnel just before it was completed.

Under the Pool Table

Few smuggling schemes have been nipped in the bud, however. One elaborate underground passageway between Douglas, Arizona, and Agua Prieta, Mexico, had been used to ship many tons of cocaine and marijuana before it was finally found. Amazed customs agents described it as being "exceptionally professionally engineered." They figured that businessman/drug smuggler Francisco Rafael Camarena had hired an architect to design it.

The tunnel was 1.5 m (5 ft.) high, 1.2 m (4 ft.) wide, and 60 m (200 ft.) long. It was reinforced with concrete and equipped with air-conditioning, electric lights, and water pumps. Along the passageway were a number of rooms, secret hatches, and nooks and crannies that runners used for stashing drugs.

At the Douglas end of the tunnel stood a warehouse owned by one of Camarena's construction businesses. At the other end was his luxury home in Agua Prieta. To enter the passageway from his house, Camarena used a special hydraulic lift. It raised the floor beneath his pool table and exposed a shaft that led to the secret tunnel.

Investigators who had been trailing shipments of illegal

drugs observed that as goods neared the Mexican-American border, they just seemed to vanish. Hunches that a tunnel must exist began to form.

Suspicious of Camarena, the investigators raided two of his properties in 1990, uncovering 1 t (2,200 lb.) of cocaine in one and 14.5 t (16 tons) in another. The "narco-tunnel" he had built to smuggle drugs into the United States was the first ever found along the Southwest border.

A Family Business

In February 2002, a hot tip led drug agents to a tunnel they claimed was "one of the most significant finds ever" along the border. For at least two or three years, a group of Mexico's most powerful and ruthless drug lords—known as the Tijuana Cartel—had been using the passage to smuggle billions of dollars worth of cocaine, marijuana, and other illegal drugs into California.

Seven brothers and four sisters in the Arellano-Felix family owned the narcotics business, headed by Benjamin Arellano-Felix. His right-hand man was brother Ramon, the most violent member of the family and a criminal on the FBI's 10 Most Wanted list. The U.S. State Department had offered a reward worth $2 million for information leading to the arrest of either man.

The Tijuana Cartel had its own security forces, well armed with automatic weapons. Its members regularly bribed officials to allow illegal drugs to travel northward, and they tortured—or killed—those who refused to cooperate. They also planned the death of anyone who used its tunnels to smuggle drugs without paying a "transportation tax." Mexican and American law enforcers held the Cartel responsible for more than 300 murders.

The hot tip received by the drug agents took them to a pig farm surrounded by a chain-link fence. Both a sign and a growling rottweiler said, "Keep Out." The rundown farm sat on scrubland close to Tecate, near California's southern border, about 13 km (8 mi.) from any main road. There, the agents anxiously searched a small house.

Breaking into a dark closet beneath a staircase, they discovered a large safe. It turned out to be empty, but the agents noticed that the closet had a false floor. Carefully prying it up, they uncovered the hidden entrance to a tunnel 6 m (20 ft.) underground and about 365 m (1,200 ft.) long.

The tunnel was lined with wood, strung with electric lights, and equipped with ventilation ducts. Railroad-style metal tracks had been installed to haul carts filled with drugs the full length of the tunnel, ending in a fireplace in a house on the other side of the border.

On the day of their search, the agents found 250 kg (550 lb.) of fresh marijuana, a sure sign that the tunnel had been used only recently. They had the passageway destroyed at once.

Drainage for Drugs

Some of the most heavily used underground smuggling routes from Mexico connect the border town of Nogales, Mexico, with Nogales, Arizona. But these tunnels weren't built for drug running.

Spanish for "walnut," Nogales in both countries was once

thick with walnut trees, but today the valley is known for its springtime flash floods. That's why the towns constructed a network of concrete-lined storm drains. Some are up to 3 m (10 ft.) tall and more than 3 m (10 ft.) wide—large enough to drive a pickup truck through!

Sections of the tunnels cross the Mexican–American border, running underground for more than 1.6 km (1 mi.) into Arizona. From the largest pipes, smugglers slink into smaller connecting ones. Greedy drug rings hire workers to dig tunnels leading from these smaller pipes to businesses or homes tucked away in the hills along the border. They create a hidden maze for moving drugs secretly into the United States.

The ringleaders reduce their chances of getting caught by keeping their workers as anonymous as possible. The tunnel diggers don't know who the smugglers are. The smugglers don't know who the drug distributors are. If captured, one group can't squeal on another.

Some runners who carry drugs through the drainage system are homeless children—as young as six! Because they live in the tunnels, they know their way around them well. And they're so desperate for money to buy food and clothes, they'll do almost anything.

These "tunnel rats," as they're called, face horrific dangers every day. Living among the sewage and slop that flow through the system, they can become seriously sick. Even worse, the rough-cut tunnels that are dug to connect with drainage pipes can collapse and bury the children alive. And adults trying to sneak under the border to live in the United States or to sell drugs sometimes beat and rob the little tunnel rats.

It's not that the Nogales drainage system isn't closely watched. Town workers inspect the underground pipes twice a week to fix any breaks. Border patrols regularly check the system, especially where it opens above ground in Arizona. And drug agents are constantly on guard. Sometimes their efforts pay off, but drug smugglers in Nogales have many different ways of moving their goods to and from the tunnels...

Lucky Breaks

In May 2000, investigators working close to the border near Nogales, Arizona, spotted something suspicious. Three men were hauling large, plastic-wrapped chests from a store that had been abandoned for a long time. They loaded the chests onto a truck and took off.

The investigators pulled the truck over to check out the load. Inside the chests, they discovered 45 packages of marijuana. When they searched the abandoned store, they found an entrance to a tunnel. The opening had been buried beneath a sleeping bag and a sheet of wood in a back room. Sure enough, the passage connected with the Nogales drainage system.

The following month, an American border patrol agent heard voices speaking through two-way radios. The sounds were coming from the Nogales drainage system. Ducking into a pipe nearby, patrol agents smelled—then spotted—seven bundles of marijuana. Someone had tied them with a rope that snaked through a hand-dug tunnel and up into the living room of a ground-floor apartment.

When the agents and the county sheriff searched the apartment, they found another 23 kg (50 lb.) of marijuana. A car parked nearby held 86 kg (190 lb.) more. The smugglers must have been hauling the drugs into the apartment when they heard someone approaching. "They boogied," the sheriff told reporters. "We interrupted their operation."

A Waiting Game

Although investigators sometimes get lucky, they often need plenty of patience to find a drug-running tunnel. In July 1999, an informant tipped off Nogales customs agents about smugglers working from a house close to the border. The agents couldn't find any evidence, but they continued to watch the house, month after month.

The following year, a drug agent dropped by to talk with a family who lived at the house. His knock went unanswered. But he noticed a lot of dirt on the windowsill—a sign that someone had been digging. He could also make out a blanket hanging behind the closed window blinds. Smugglers often use blankets as "blackout curtains."

The agent reported his suspicions, and the Nogales sewer department was called in to check out the drainage pipe near the home. Workers stuck a robotic camera inside the pipe to see what was there. It traveled along until something stopped it in its tracks. It couldn't move any farther.

A drug agent volunteered to enter the drainage system. He squirmed his way for 150 m (500 ft.) through a pipe only 60 cm (2 ft.) in diameter until he was blocked by a tangle of string and batteries. Pushing through, he came to a large metal lid, its hinge welded to the pipe. He opened it and found himself in a crude tunnel that looked as if it had been hacked out with a pick and shovel. It ran for 8 m (26 ft.) with a line of bare lightbulbs to light the way.

The tunnel ended in the very house the agents had been watching. There, they were rewarded for their patience. They found 198 bricks of cocaine, weighing a total of 380 kg (840 lb.) and worth nearly $6 million to the smugglers.

Where Will It End?

During 2002, law enforcers managed to strike three heavy blows against Mexico's largest drug-smuggling ring, the Tijuana Cartel. Mexican police killed kingpin Ramon Arellano-Felix in a shootout and later arrested his brother Benjamin, the Cartel's leader. And following a two-year investigation called Operation Vice Grip, American investigators cracked four drug distribution rings that were closely linked to the Cartel.

"We have seriously damaged a large, sophisticated, and very violent drug-trafficking organization," exclaimed one California lawyer.

But have they defeated it? A Tijuana magazine editor whom the Cartel tried to assassinate said, "You cut off a branch if one Arellano dies or another is captured, but the family will always grow new branches."

That's just what appears to be happening. The family's youngest brother, college graduate Francisco Arellano-Felix— nicknamed "Little Tiger"—is taking charge of the Tijuana Cartel, with help from his physician brother Eduardo and accountant sister Enedina. Some officials believe that the Cartel will be less brutal under its new leadership. Still, it will continue to hire countless numbers of drug runners to do its dirty work.

Like other smuggling rings in this billion-dollar industry, it will keep attracting desperate people willing to pack their bodies with drugs and cross the border through danger-filled tunnels.

Escape from Libby

Packed in tight rows to conserve heat and space, the men lay down to sleep—a hard, bare floor their only bed. Here and there, someone pulled a thin blanket across his chest. But most of the soldiers had no protection from the wintry winds that blew through the barred windows.

Sleep didn't come easy. Shivering from the cold and aching with hunger, the men lay wondering who would be dead come morning...who would be tossed into a rough board box...who would be carted away in an open wagon.

Even as prisons go, Libby was dreadful. During the American Civil War (1861-1865), the Union of northern states and the Confederacy of southern states were fighting over important issues, such as the right to own slaves, and overall federal control versus state power. The Confederates opened Libby in Richmond, Virginia, to hold prisoners of war—specifically, Union officers.

The prison was terribly crowded, with 1,200 prisoners, sometimes more, stuffed into six large rooms. There, each man had little more than 2 m² (22 sq. ft.) of space. Officers were called "fresh fish" when they first arrived at Libby. They were crammed in like sardines in a can.

Libby prisoners received only scanty rations of food, often

just a bit of soup or corn bread. "I entered the prison weighing 160 pounds [73 kg]," reported one survivor, "and came out weighing less than 90 [41 kg]."

Then there were the rats. Hundreds of them. They infested the prison. Straw piled knee-deep on the floor of a cellar storage room made perfect nesting material for the rodents. The prisoners called the room "Rat Hell," but neither the public nor the press believed them. A newspaper reporter for the Richmond *Sentinel* wrote, "If rats exist at all, they are brought there by the prisoners themselves, among whom are many whose naturally filthy habits preclude them from being free of such pests."

Danger was an everyday reality at Libby. Armed guards watched the prison windows and the outer doors closely. They were prepared to shoot—without warning—anyone who attempted to escape. Some guards fired their guns through the windows just for "sport," once killing a prisoner instantly as he read. To head off any rescue attempts, the building itself was salted with explosives. Guards were ordered to blow it up immediately if enemy troops so much as entered the city of Richmond.

In all, the harsh conditions at Libby Prison claimed countless lives during the Civil War, which pitted American against American. Losses on both sides were heavy. But the number of Union soldiers who died as prisoners of war in Confederate jails such as Libby was more than twice the number who died in battle!

Enter Rose and Hamilton

It was to this bleak Confederate prison that Colonel Thomas Rose, commander of the 77th Pennsylvania Infantry, was taken on October 1, 1863. After losing a battle in Georgia, he limped into Libby, convinced his only chance for survival lay in breaking out. A prison term almost surely meant death from exposure, starvation, infection, or gunshot.

Rose soon found a partner in his desperate mission. Searching Libby Prison for possible escape routes, he met another soldier who was doing the same thing. Captain Andrew Hamilton of the Federal 12th Kentucky Cavalry had arrived at Libby just two days before Rose. The two officers decided to team up.

"Our acquaintance ripened into a mutual friendship," said Hamilton, "and we soon had the full confidence of each other."

Rose and Hamilton knew breaking out of Libby wouldn't be easy. The prison stood alone near the bottom of a hill, close to a canal and a river. Three sides of the jail faced vacant lots, which offered no cover for escapees.

Libby Prison was made up of three brick buildings with connecting doorways. It had been hurriedly converted to a jail for prisoners of war in 1861. One of the buildings had previously been used to supply equipment for ships. So suddenly did it change hands that its sign, "L. Libby & Sons, Ship Chandlers and Grocers," remained, giving the jail its name.

Each building in Libby had three stories, plus a basement. The prisoners occupied the top two floors. On the main level, there were offices, rooms for the guards, a small one-room hospital, and a kitchen with an eating area. The cellar, dark and damp, was used mostly for storage, but it also contained a carpenter's shop, a few cells, and a second kitchen.

Shortly after Rose and Hamilton arrived at Libby, the guards made the cellar completely off limits—probably to reduce any chance of escape. Stairways and trapdoors heading down from the main floor were boarded shut. All prisoners then had to use the kitchen on the main floor to heat their soup.

Fireplace Passage

Rose and Hamilton figured the best way to escape from Libby was to tunnel out, so their first challenge was to find a way into the cellar (see diagram). That led them to the kitchen on the main floor. Besides their sleeping quarters, it was the only room they had access to, and guards seldom checked it at night.

The officers figured they could create a passage starting from the back of the kitchen fireplace. If they worked carefully, they might avoid breaking through the wall and into the hospital on the other side. The passage would extend downward—curving under the hospital floor and into Rat Hell in the cellar. Of course, the passage had to be wide enough for a man to pass through. Building it would be tricky.

One night, while their comrades slept, Rose and Hamilton slipped into the kitchen and quietly moved aside one of two stoves that stood in front of the fireplace. Working in the dark, they swept the soot and ashes onto a blanket. Rose acted as the lookout, while Hamilton used an old knife to scrape away some of the mortar. With patience, he managed to pry out a few bricks.

By early morning, the men had to stop working. They carefully set the bricks that Hamilton had removed back into place. Then they scooped up soot and ashes to fill in the cracks and smeared the fireplace to hide their handiwork. After replacing the stove, they sneaked back to their resting spots on the

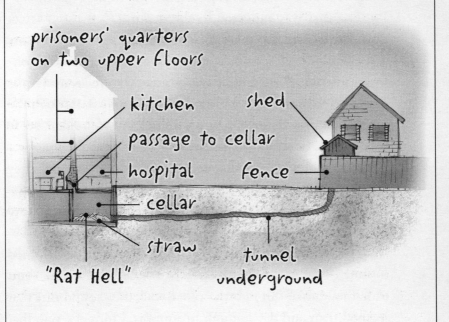

Escape Route from Libby Prison

prisoners' quarters on two upper floors

kitchen

shed

passage to cellar

hospital

fence

cellar

straw

"Rat Hell"

tunnel underground

floor above. Sleep was brief, however. They had to appear for roll call at 9:00 a.m.

After the 12th night of hard work, they completed the passage to the cellar. Rose and Hamilton were wild with joy. Still, the big job—digging a tunnel to the outside world—lay ahead of them.

Tunnels One, Two, and Three

The job turned out to be even tougher than the officers first imagined. In the end, they began not one tunnel, but three!

The first was expected to run 4.5 m (15 ft.) to a sewer pipe. From there, the men hoped to escape to the river. Rose and Hamilton enlisted a few other prisoners to help them construct the tunnel. By scraping away mortar from around some of the bricks in the cellar, they managed to break through the wall. Then they began digging a tunnel, but it flooded. Rose ordered it refilled and abandoned.

Almost at once, the diggers started a second tunnel. They made another hole through the cellar wall, but soon hit the huge logs that formed the building's foundation. They were forced to abandon this tunnel as well.

The officers were discouraged, but they were determined to find a way out. After all, they had little to lose. The third time they broke through the cellar wall, they found dirt that seemed firm and dry enough to support a tunnel—one that would not lead to the foundation logs.

The new plan was to dig a passage at least 15 m (50 ft.) in length—long enough to run beneath a vacant lot next to the prison, under a fence, and into a small carriage shed. From there, the men could escape whenever the coast was clear.

Team Work

Rose organized three teams of five men each, including Hamilton and himself. He scheduled every team to work one night out of three. So they could move more easily through the kitchen fireplace passage to the cellar, Hamilton created a ladder from some thick rope that one of the officers had scavenged from the guards.

Other than their own hands and fingers, the diggers had few tools to work with: small knives, chisels stolen from the carpenter's shop in the cellar, candles for light, a bit of rope, and wooden spittoons provided for tobacco-chewers to spit in.

For the tunneling job, a digger would tie two pieces of rope around one of the spittoons and drag it along as he worked. After he filled it with dirt, he'd yank on the rope that led back to the tunnel entrance. There an officer hauled it out and emptied it, hiding the dirt under the thick straw that covered the floor of Rat Hell.

The third person on the team fanned his hat near the entrance, moving air so the diggers could breathe, and their candles would burn. A fourth was the lookout, ready to signal the others at any sign of danger. And the fifth man was a substitute, called in to work when one of his teammates was unwell or had trouble sneaking away in the night to work on the tunnel.

As each team completed a shift, they hid their precious tools in the cellar and climbed the passage to the kitchen. There, they replaced the fireplace bricks, covering them with soot and ashes, and moved the stove back into place.

Trouble!

The project did not go smoothly. In the darkness of the large cellar, the men found it hard to figure out where they were going. They could speak only in whispers, so they depended mostly on touch to find one another. Rose sometimes had to round up men who were lost.

Bad air was another hazard. Breathing was so exhausting that the diggers seldom had the strength to crawl out of the tunnel. Often they had to be pulled out by the others.

Rats made matters even worse. At night, they seemed to be everywhere. As Hamilton reported, "Hundreds of them squealed while they ran over the diggers, almost without a sign of fear."

No wonder the teams sometimes fell apart. For a few nights, progress on the tunnel stopped altogether. But the men must have wondered how long they could survive inside Libby's walls, for they soon reassembled and went back to work.

After a couple of weeks, one of the tunnelers had a heart-stopping experience. At approximately 1:00 a.m., Captain W.S.B. Randall of the 2nd Ohio Infantry was digging deep inside the tunnel when he was ordered to open it up to the surface. Rose thought the underground passageway had gone far enough and must already have passed beneath the fence. He was wrong.

"I broke through on the side next to a guard, close up to the fence," wrote Randall after his escape. "The guard heard me burst through the surface. He left his beat and came and stood right astride my face, leaned on the fence and looked over into the enclosed yard. He thought the noise was over the fence. He stood there, I suppose, for about half a minute. It seemed like half a century to me. Great drops of cold sweat stood out on my forehead; I couldn't breathe; the events of my life seemed to flit before me, and I lived ages in a moment's time. But he did not see me, and went away."

Luckily for the tunnelers, the guard probably thought he'd heard rats. Randall hastily stuffed his dirt-covered overalls into the hole. The team soon extended the tunnel under the fence, then opened it up into the shed. Done!

Goodbye, Libby

The next evening—February 9, 1864—the officers prepared to flee the prison. Dressed in civilian clothes sent to them by family and friends, the men pocketed pieces of bread they'd saved, plus bits of dried meat.

Randall packed along an extra treasure, a bottle of cayenne pepper he'd received hidden inside a roll of butter. It later proved invaluable, putting the enemy's bloodhounds off his scent as they searched for escaped prisoners.

"Freedom was within our grasp and thoughts of home and loved ones came thick and fast," reported Hamilton. By then, he'd managed to survive more than four months behind the walls of Libby.

That night, all the men in the prison crammed into the kitchen and eating area, where they played loud music and danced. Most of them had only recently heard about the secret tunnel and the escape plans. Their job was to distract the guards and provide cover while the first 30 escapees removed bricks from the fireplace and slipped through the passage to the cellar.

"It was a living drama: dancing in one part of the room, dark shadows disappearing through the chimney in another part," noted Colonel Harrison Hobart, of the 21st Wisconsin. Rose and Hamilton had put him in charge of organizing the escape of the others after the first group had fled.

The plan, according to Hamilton, was that each of the 15 men who had dug the tunnel would pick a friend to break out with. After those 30 men had left, Hobart would close the kitchen entrance to the passage to give them time to get away. The next night, he was supposed to let more prisoners leave through the tunnel.

Once in the darkness of the cellar, the first group of escapees was overcome with fear at the thought of crawling through the narrow tunnel to a fate unknown. So terrified were they, that Randall later wrote, "Our parting in that old cellar will never be forgotten until the last one of that little party is laid away in the grave."

The tunnel was 2.5 m (8 ft.) underground and barely big enough to creep through. In places, it was so tight that some of the men had to remove their outer clothes and shove them ahead as they crawled. Pushing against the tunnel floor with their feet and grasping the walls with their fingers, the men edged forward, bit by bit.

When they reached the carriage shed, they wriggled out and checked around cautiously before making a break for it. Some of the men ducked through a yard to the cover of an arched driveway, then entered the street from there. Usually traveling in twos on that dark night, they tried to blend in calmly with the citizens of Richmond.

Inside Libby, however, the evening did not go as planned. From the windows, many of the prisoners spotted their comrades going free. Crazy with excitement, they rushed to the chimney, pushing and shoving to get out.

Instead of waiting until the next night, Hobart managed to hold the men back for only about an hour. Another 79 prisoners, including Hobart himself, crept down the passage and out through the tunnel before dawn.

The Fallout

The next day, roll call in Libby Prison lasted nearly four hours as amazed guards discovered that 109 of the Union officers were missing. The final total would probably have been much greater if the prisoners had stayed calm and followed the original escape plan.

Guards searched Libby high and low, but at first they failed to find the prisoners' route to freedom. The tunnel's cellar entrance had been hidden by rocks. Officials concluded that the guards had accepted bribes and placed them under arrest. But a more thorough search of the prison revealed both the passage from the main floor to the cellar and the tunnel to the outdoors.

A Richmond newspaper described the escape as extraordinary. "It is fortunate that the leak was discovered when it was," the report claimed, "or the exodus would have been continued night after night until there would have been no Yankees [Union officers] to guard."

In less than three days, search parties recaptured 48 of the escaped prisoners of war, including Rose. Another 2 were found drowned. Hamilton, Randall, and Hobart were among 59 soldiers who reached the North safely.

The recaptured prisoners were sent back to Libby, where guards locked them in dark, crowded cells for days. "Imagine our filthiness when we were let out more dead than alive, of what we fully expected would be our grave," commented one.

Still, Colonel Thomas Rose, the mastermind behind the clever escape, managed to survive the rest of his stay in Libby Prison and see the Union win the American Civil War in 1865.

As for the building itself, it reverted to a fertilizer store-house until it was "rediscovered" by a businessman from Chicago, Illinois. In 1889, he arranged to have Libby Prison moved to his city as a tourist attraction. Timber by timber and brick by brick, the building was taken apart and shipped off in 132 boxcars.

Along the way, the train derailed, and onlookers swooped in to grab pieces of the prison as souvenirs. Still, most of it reached Chicago, where it was reassembled and put on display. A sign marked a hole in the wall as the escape tunnel entrance, but the hole was in the wrong place.

As interest in the prison faded, Libby was taken apart once more in 1899. Its owners kept only one wall, incorporating it into a larger wall of a huge coliseum they built on the site. Eighty years later, that building was torn down, and the few bricks and a door that remained of Libby Prison were moved to a museum. They were all that was left of the dreadful Confederate jail that held Union officers captive during the American Civil War.

Wednesday, March 24, 1999. The early morning rain clouds had lifted, and warm breezes were blowing through the Alps. What had begun as a pleasant, rather ordinary day would soon turn into a nightmare—one that many would remember for a lifetime.

At exactly 10:46 a.m., a 57-year-old trucker, Gilbert Degraves from Belgium, reached the French end of a long highway tunnel that led across the border to Italy. He was hauling a refrigerated semitrailer loaded down with 12 t (13 tons) of flour and 9 t (10 tons) of margarine. For him, it was just a routine trip.

Degraves stopped at the tollgate, then steered his big rig carefully into the tunnel and picked up speed. Soon he noticed drivers in the oncoming traffic flashing their headlights at him. Checking in his rearview mirror, he spotted smoke! It appeared to be coming from the right side of his rig.

Immediately, Degraves slowed down and pulled off the road into a rest area marked "21." At that point, he was little more than halfway through the tunnel. He hopped out just as smoke started to pour from his truck and noticed more smoke was rising between the truck and the semitrailer. He was reaching under the driver's seat for his fire extinguisher, when all of a sudden the truck burst into flames.

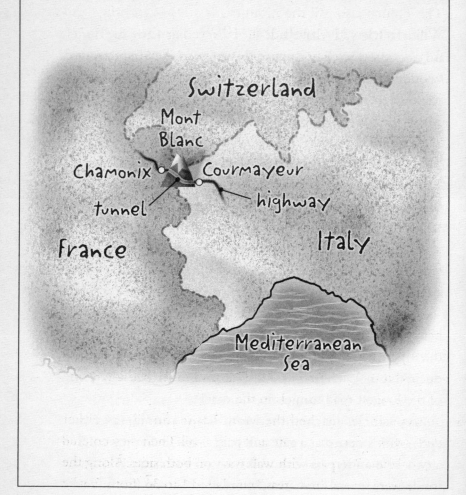

Location of
Mont Blanc Tunnel

Switzerland

Mont
Blanc

Chamonix

Courmayeur

tunnel

highway

France

Italy

Mediterranean
Sea

"It exploded!" he later told reporters. "There was no time to grab the fire extinguisher. Everything was ablaze in half a minute."

Route through the Mountain

Vehicles carrying vacationers, truckers, and local residents poured into the tunnel through Mont Blanc in a steady stream. The French also call the mountain *La Dame Blanche*—the White Lady—and what a lady she is. Towering 4,807 m (15,771 ft.) above sea level, her upper slopes are cloaked year-round with thick blankets of snow. Her lower slopes are densely wooded and slashed with fast-flowing streams and waterfalls. And she spans three separate countries: France, Italy, and Switzerland.

The Mont Blanc tunnel is an important section of one of Europe's busiest highways. It links two resort towns: Courmayeur, Italy, and Chamonix, France—site of the first Winter Olympics, in 1924 (see map). People from around the world flock to the area to ski, mountain climb, hike, and sight-see. They ride its gondolas and cable cars and take trips on a steep railroad to Mont Blanc's most famous glacier, *Mer de Glace*.

The mountain tunnel was built to ease the flow of traffic between France and Italy—to create a faster way to get past the Alps. After years of digging from both sides, the countries opened it in 1965. At 11.6 km (7.2 mi.) in length, it was one of the longest road tunnels in the world.

As vehicles reached the Mont Blanc tunnel—at either end—they stopped at a gate and paid a toll. Then they entered a two-lane underpass with walkways on both sides. Along the inside were several "rest areas," numbered 1 to 36 (from France to Italy). Motorists used them as places to pull off the road if their vehicles broke down, ran out of gas, or blew a tire. For emergency use, every second rest area contained a safety shelter that provided fresh air and helped shield people from fire. Other emergency equipment included fire extinguishers, alarm pullboxes, and telephones.

Where There's Smoke...

Just as Degraves was pulling his truck off the road, a control operator at the French tollgate noticed smoke appearing on the monitor screens that displayed images from security cameras throughout the tunnel.

But by then, several other vehicles had already followed Degraves past the gate: one pickup truck, eighteen large trucks, nine passenger vehicles, and a motorcycle. Having no idea of the danger ahead, the drivers continued until they screeched to a halt behind the burning truck. At that point, motorists near the back of the line were not even able to see any flames. Some of them must have felt impatient, wondering what was causing the hold-up.

Degraves's fuel tank, which held about 550 l (120 gal.) of diesel at the time, was soon bolstering the blaze. Flames spread quickly, moving from the truck to the semitrailer. There they fed furiously on the huge mass of melting margarine it contained.

"I ran for my life," said Degraves, who wasted no more time near his vehicle. Instead, he took off down the tunnel toward the Italian gate.

Four of the truckers caught behind the fire immediately pulled out and steered daringly around it. The rest of the vehicles remained tightly packed behind the flames and fast-thickening walls of smoke. To make matters worse, the lighting system in the fire area was destroyed within minutes, plunging motorists into total darkness and causing short circuits that shut down the fire sprinklers.

At the Italian gate, the control station received an emergency call and a fire pullbox alarm from someone at rest area #22. But by then, it was too late to stop eight trucks with semi-trailers and several passenger vehicles from entering the tunnel.

As heavy smoke appeared on the screens of the control monitors in both countries, sirens went off at the gates. All further traffic heading for the tunnel was stopped at 10:55 a.m. —nine minutes after Degraves first entered it.

Like an Oven

Fires can turn tunnels into huge ovens, pulling in air from one end and pushing it out the other. The flames can spread rapidly. In fact, if tunnel fires aren't conquered within the first 15 minutes, they can easily rage out of control. Although many of Mont Blanc's previous fires had been small enough to be snuffed out with fire extinguishers, this one was burning hard and fast.

Besides growing swiftly, tunnel fires burn long and hot, and the fire in Mont Blanc was no different. Temperatures in parts of the tunnel soon shot above 1,000°C (1,800°F)—10 times the temperature of boiling water! As the flames engulfed vehicle after vehicle, they twisted the metal bodies, exploded rubber tires, and melted the asphalt on the road beneath them.

Rescue Attempts

As soon as the French gate was closed to traffic, a tunnel agent hurried into the tunnel. However, he wasn't able to get near the burning truck in rest area #21. In fact, he came no closer than area #18.

Minutes later, the tunnel's fire engines charged past the gate, but they barely got as far as rest area #17. The smoke was so dense the firefighters could see nothing, and they had to flee to a shelter to escape overwhelming heat and the toxins— including carbon monoxide—that filled the air.

At 11:10 a.m., a rescue vehicle arrived from Chamonix but was blocked at rest area #12. Its engine died from lack of oxygen. At 11:36, another was stopped at #5. Several of the firefighters became trapped in the tunnel, and rescue efforts then included helping them escape.

Meanwhile, at the Italian gate, a patrol officer plunged into the tunnel just after the alarm went off. He managed to get within a few meters of the Belgian truck. In fact, he was the only rescuer who actually saw the vehicle on fire. At that moment—11:05 a.m.—he still believed that it might have been possible for firefighters to beat the blaze. Black smoke and intense heat, however, changed his mind.

As the patrol officer made his way back, he met Italian crews who had been trying desperately to reach the flaming truck. Together, they turned their attention to helping motorists flee the scene.

Firefighters arriving from Courmayeur also failed to reach the source of the fire, even traveling by foot. Blinded by the smoke, they had to turn back. Five of them ducked into a safety shelter and were later rescued through an air duct that led to it. As in France, the rescuers were defeated by high temperatures, thick smoke, and toxic gases. Retreat was the only way to ensure their own survival.

Disaster!

The fire in the Mont Blanc tunnel burned for more than 50 hours. Working from the Italian end, emergency forces gradually made their way deeper and deeper into the tunnel, spraying the walls to cool them down.

Large sections of the tunnel were heavily damaged. Parts of the ceiling and walls had peeled and cracked. Chunks of concrete and loads that were being hauled by trucks blocked the passage. Crews had to use heavy machinery to plow and dig their way through.

Everywhere, the foul smell of fumes and burnt rubber hung in the air and clung to the rescuers' clothes as they worked. Smoke blackened their faces and rose from their gear even when they left the tunnel on breaks.

Eventually, the firefighters managed to douse all the vehicles attacked by flames. By Friday, they had traveled the full length of tunnel.

As news reporters peppered them with questions, members of the crew couldn't find a voice to speak. "The firefighters are in shock, especially those who went in first," a commander explained. "The vehicles are totally destroyed—just twisted wrecks."

So what happened to the many truckers, skiers, hikers, and local residents who were caught inside Mont Blanc?

The Fortunate

The travelers who had entered the tunnel from the Italian gate were the lucky ones. The air was flowing toward France, carrying much of the smoke and toxic gas in that direction. As people retreated from the fire toward Italy, they headed toward cleaner and clearer air. With help from one another and the rescuers, every one of them escaped!

The eight truckers who had driven into the tunnel just before the Italian alarm went off had soon spotted the heavy black smoke. The tunnel was too narrow to allow them to turn their trucks around, but they quickly abandoned them and ran.

One of the drivers told newspaper reporters, "A fellow trucker called me on my CB radio and told me to stop and turn back as there was a fire." He had immediately headed for a safety shelter. From inside, he could hear car horns honking and people screaming.

Fortunately, the drivers of all the passenger vehicles caught behind these trucks had been able to make U-turns and drive to safety.

The four truckers who had entered the Mont Blanc tunnel from France and had dared to drive around the burning truck managed to reach Italy alive. And Gilbert Degraves, driver of the burning Belgian truck, also escaped through the tunnel to Italy. Along the way, he met a patrol officer who assisted him.

"In a few minutes, the tunnel was like an oven," Degraves said after his narrow escape. "I've been extremely lucky."

The Unfortunate

The drivers trapped behind the burning truck had tried to turn around and head back to France, but they could barely see through the smoke, and the low levels of oxygen in the tunnel soon stalled their engines. Most of the motorists remained in their vehicles; some joined others where they huddled together in one car. Still others, including two truckers, tried to flee on foot, but they didn't get far before smoke overcame them.

A few motorists made their way into fire-resistant shelters in rest areas and phoned the French control station. But soon, the copper wires that connected them melted away, cutting them off from hope. The fire's heat became too intense for the shelters to protect the motorists for long.

One Italian tunnel employee, who happened to be at the French gate that awful morning, had driven his motorcycle into the tunnel and come across people trying to escape the fire by foot. He urged them to move along the wall that had fresh air outlets. Then he drove deeper into the tunnel.

Around him, lights and cables were tumbling from the ceiling. He returned to the French gate to report the chaos, then bravely reentered the tunnel. Survivors describing his heroism say he helped save the lives of at least 10 people that day.

The motorcyclist kept in touch with his control station by radio for about an hour. But as the smoke and heat became too great, he dumped his motorcycle near rest area #20. Sadly, he died alongside one of the drivers. The frame of his motorcycle was found 200 m (655 ft.) from where the fire first began. The heat had melted it into the pavement.

Investigators think that smoke and toxic gases—not extreme heat and flames—were likely the main killers. If so, many of the victims would have died within the first 15 minutes.

In all, the Mont Blanc tunnel fire claimed the lives of 38 motorists that day. The list of victims included five members of one French family and an Italian family of four returning from a dentist appointment in Chamonix. Shortly after the fire, a member of the Chamonix Fire Brigade died from the effects of the smoke, raising the grim total to 39 deaths.

Could any of these lives have been saved? No one really knows. But one thing is sure: There was no lack of courage among those who tried to rescue the victims, despite soaring temperatures, blinding smoke, and poisonous gases. Memories of their bravery live on at the Mont Blanc tunnel.

Three Years Later

It wasn't until March 9, 2002—almost three full years after the fire—that wheels once again rolled through the Mont Blanc tunnel. Based on studies by investigators, tunnel operators realized they could do more to protect motorists. They rebuilt the long passageway and added a number of safety features, including an escape corridor beneath the road. They also set up a system of barriers that would help stop traffic as soon as any crisis occurred. And they stationed firefighters—permanently—at the middle and both ends of the tunnel.

The passageway was reopened to traffic very gradually. In March, only passenger cars were allowed to use it. They were followed in April by small trucks and tourist buses, and in May by larger trucks. Near the end of June, the first of the big rigs and their loads began passing through. But any vehicle carrying hazardous cargo has been banned.

As traffic started to flow through the Mont Blanc tunnel

again, thousands of protesters turned out. They weren't opposed to cars using the corridor, but they were concerned that big rigs and their loads would be safety hazards. When protesters blocked the first heavy freight truck that arrived at the tunnel, they discovered it was Belgian—like the semitrailer that started the inferno in 1999—so they set its contents on fire. Police were called in to clear the way for the big rigs. And although these large trucks continue to use the tunnel, memories and stories of the fire will surely haunt motorists for many years to come.

Courage Under Water

Go back in time—more than 100 years. You're sitting in a stiff, waterproof suit. On your feet are lead-weighted, 9-kg (20-lb.) boots. A 27-kg (60-lb.) brass helmet is placed over your head, leaving you to peer out through a thick glass "porthole." The helmet screws onto a metal breastplate—another 18 kg (40 lb.) of gear—over your suit.

Wearing this standard diving equipment, you plunge into the water. A long, heavy hose delivers every breath of air you take. It's pumped down to your helmet from the surface. Awkward as it is, you must somehow manage to maneuver through and under tight spaces without getting stuck or tangled. What's more, you are forced to operate in total darkness. You have no form of underwater light.

You've just walked a few steps in the boots of Alexander Lambert, one of the greatest divers who ever lived. He wasn't a very tall man, but he had a chest like a barrel, a muscular neck, and powerful arms and legs. His strength, skill, and courage as a diver are the stuff of legends.

During the 1880s, a company named Great Western Railway hired Lambert to work under conditions so tricky they could easily have cost him his life. Instead, his brave efforts made possible the construction of an amazing tunnel beneath the Severn estuary in Great Britain. In its day, it was truly a wonder: the longest submarine tunnel anywhere in the world!

The Severn Challenge

The estuary of the lengthy River Severn enters Bristol Channel, a wide arm of the Atlantic that separates South Wales from southwestern England. Funnel-shaped, the estuary experiences tides of more than 12 m (39 ft.)—second in height only to the world-famous tides in Canada's Bay of Fundy. In spite of the tides, heavy loads of coal had to be carted to market across the Severn by boat. The only alternative was to haul them by train along a roundabout route over steep tracks. Not an easy task.

In the 1860s and 1870s, coal mining in South Wales was booming, so demands for an easier, more reliable route to southwestern England swelled. Eager to win a greater share of the coal business, railroad companies competed to find better ways to cross the Severn.

Some decided to build a bridge despite the high costs and the risk of ships striking its supports in foggy weather. Great Western Railway chose to go under—rather than over—the estuary. Its engineers figured that tunneling beneath the Severn would be cheaper and safer than building over it, but they knew it wouldn't be simple.

Although the engineers picked a site where the estuary narrowed, the tunnel would still have to be more than 7 km (4 mi.) long. And it would have to lie beneath the "Shoots," a steep gully about 15 m (50 ft.) deeper than most of the estuary. That meant the tunnel would have to angle downward to a point more than 43 m (140 ft.) below the level of the railroad tracks on either side of the Severn. And to allow for train traffic, it had to be 7.5 m (24.5 ft.) tall and 8 m (26 ft.) wide. In all, the tunnel beneath the Severn would be an engineering marvel!

Getting on with It

Great Western Railway began construction in 1873 (see diagram). On the edge of the Welsh side of the estuary, crews sank a vertical shaft 61 m (200 ft.) deep. Miners were lowered to the bottom of the shaft, where they started working eastward, digging a section of the tunnel that passed directly under the Severn. In round-the-clock shifts, they drilled and blasted their way slowly through hard rock.

Occasionally, water broke in, gushing through the passage, so the miners constructed a wall 2 m (6 ft.) thick some distance into the tunnel from the shaft. Engineers thought it would head off any serious flooding. An iron door in the wall could be shut, sealing off the rest of the passage until the water was pumped out.

The system worked well. More shafts were sunk on both sides of the estuary and the tunnel grew, section by section. Some miners worked eastward; others, westward. After more than six years of labor, it looked as if two of the long sections beneath the estuary would soon be joined. They were only 153 m (500 ft.) apart.

The Great Spring

Then came trouble. As the miners on the Welsh side were digging a passage angling up from the tunnel's lowest point, they struck water. Not just a trickle or two, but a powerful, surging

Great Western Railway Tunnel

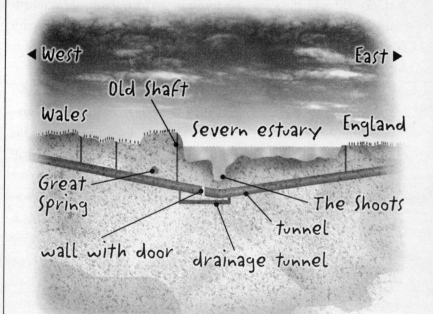

West ◄

East ►

Old Shaft

Wales

Severn estuary

England

Great
Spring

The Shoots

wall with door

drainage tunnel

tunnel

wave! Jamming timbers across the passageway, the men struggled heroically to hold it back, but the water continued to roar in. It surged down the passage toward the first and deepest shaft, the "Old Shaft," where it tumbled into a drainage tunnel.

In no time at all, the drainage tunnel overflowed, but at least it gave the miners a chance to escape. And they did. Surprisingly, there was no loss of life.

The water continued to pour in at a rate of about 1,630,000 l (360,000 gal.) an hour—far too furiously for the tunnel's pumps to handle. Within hours, long passageways were completely submerged, and water had risen up the shafts to the level of the tides.

The floodwater was fresh and clear. Ironically, it was not coming from the estuary, which engineers and miners feared might flood the tunnel one day. Instead, it was rising from somewhere underground. The miners named it the "Great Spring."

To pump out the huge volume of water, the company had to bring in much stronger machinery. All mining operations were halted while engine houses were built to serve the massive new pumps.

Meanwhile, Great Western tried to stop the flow temporarily. The company built two oak shields, weighing about 2.5 t (3 tons) each, to block the entrances to two of the passages. These enormous plugs had to be lowered down the Old Shaft to the tunnel, then wedged tightly into place—a job that could only be done underwater.

Calling Alexander Lambert

Great Western Railway hired a team of skilled ocean divers,

headed by British expert Alexander Lambert. The team depended on people at the surface to pump them air and control its flow. It was risky. Too much air could force the divers to rise so fast that the nitrogen in their bodies could damage their blood vessels—even kill them. Too little, and they would suffer serious lung damage.

Underwater, the divers had to find their way in total darkness, fumbling around overturned platforms and the scattered tools miners had been using to build the tunnel. A single careless move in all that clutter could sever an air hose, leaving a diver with no air to breathe.

So great was the water pressure in the tunnel that the diving team was left with little energy to work. The pumps in the shaft had to be reactivated and more water removed. Then Lambert and the others struggled for about two weeks to maneuver the gigantic shields into place.

Just as success seemed close, one of the shields began to leak. The divers managed to pass several bags of cement through a small opening in the oak plug and seal the shield in place.

Still, there were more failures, and the divers were sent on missions to solve problems such as broken seals. At one point, the force from a single pump was so great that it sucked Lambert—as strong as he was—against its inlet pipe and held him prisoner there. It took three brawny men to yank him free!

Closing the Door: Strike One

Despite the initial successes of the divers, the tunnel flooded again whenever the pumps were stopped. It wasn't until October 1880—one full year after the Great Spring first burst in—that Great Western discovered why they hadn't been able to block the flow of water. The iron door in the wall that had been built to divide the passage and control flooding was standing open. In their panic, the fleeing miners had neglected to close it behind them! If the door could be shut, the company believed it could stop the flooding. Clearly, it was another job for ace diver Alexander Lambert.

This time, his mission would take him 300 m (985 ft.) from the base of the Old Shaft. There, he had to close the heavy door, then walk the long distance back to the shaft.

Two other divers would be on hand to help direct and safeguard Lambert's air hose. One would be stationed near the bottom of the shaft, and the other would stand halfway along the passage. In the inky darkness of the tunnel, the three could not see one another. Nor could they communicate.

Carrying only a short iron bar, Lambert scrambled over and around stacks of rubble, mining instruments, even some overturned carts and trucks. Bit by bit, he groped his way through the tunnel, often stopping to heave heavy rocks and fallen timber aside.

After covering about nine-tenths of the distance, Lambert was brought to a sudden stop. His air hose had wound and twisted its way around too many posts and piles. There was no more to let out, and he was forced to turn back.

The return trip was tortuous. Lambert had no way of alerting his assistants to start drawing in the long air hose. Instead, he had to wind his way back, slowly untangling his hose and coiling it up so he could lug it along. The mission to shut the door was a failure—this time.

Closing the Door: Strike Two

Defeated by his own air hose, Lambert was keen to hear about an underwater breathing system that had just been invented by British seaman Henry Fleuss. It freed divers from their long hoses completely. The invention—called a rebreather—consisted of a waterproof mask linked by two rubber tubes to a bag worn on a diver's back. A lightweight copper tank supplied pure oxygen to the bag.

A diver used his nose to inhale oxygen from one tube and his mouth to exhale carbon dioxide through the other. A chemical in the bag absorbed most of the carbon dioxide, and the diver breathed in recycled oxygen. When this oxygen was almost used up, the diver released some pure oxygen from the tank into the bag. The rebreather allowed divers to spend up to three hours underwater.

Great Western invited Fleuss to test out his invention in the flooded Severn tunnel. Even though he was not an experienced diver, he tried his best to reach the open door. As soon as he headed into the tunnel, however, he grew confused and lost his sense of direction. Sometimes crawling over garbage, sometimes sinking into the mucky floor, he gave up before long and resurfaced. So awful was the ordeal that he vowed he would never again enter the tunnel.

At Great Western's suggestion, Lambert borrowed the rebreather from Fleuss and decided to try his luck with it. "I'll give her a go," he said simply.

Fleuss warned him to watch his step. By brushing against rough timber or twisted rails, he could easily tear the rebreather bag. Of course, that would leave him helpless to return safely to the surface.

There were other dangers, too—ones that Fleuss and Lambert knew nothing about at the time. Breathing pure oxygen under heavy pressure is toxic. It can cause lung irritations, convulsions—even death.

With the rebreather strapped into place, Lambert cautiously descended the shaft, entered the tunnel, and managed to get all the way to the open door. He found two heavy steel rails blocking the entrance. Taking care not to damage his breathing bag, he struggled with the rails and managed to lift one of them out of the way. But the other, he couldn't budge. After a 90-minute dive, he felt defeated once more.

Closing the Door: Home Run!

Down, but not out, Lambert was willing to take a third stab at closing the door and giving the pumps a chance to drain the tunnel. But he had to wait another two days while Fleuss went to London to pick up a new supply of oxygen and some carbon dioxide absorbers for his invention.

When the rebreather had been refilled and readied, Lambert headed straight back into the tunnel. This time, he carried a crowbar. Very carefully, he maneuvered his way to the doorway, pried up the second rail, and pushed the door shut! Even today, professional divers describe this feat as one of the greatest achievements in diving. Back at the surface, Lambert announced his success with both pride and relief.

Soon the pumps were running again. And four weeks later, the pump foreman was able to enter the tunnel himself, turn off a valve, and start work on further flood controls. By early January 1881, the Great Spring appeared to be contained.

Replay

Alexander Lambert hadn't heard the last from Great Western Railway. In 1883, the company experienced yet another serious setback. As the evening shift was cleaning up rubble following a day's blasting, water suddenly swept into the tunnel. The Great Spring, imprisoned for nearly three years, had broken out once more.

Miners and steel rails bobbed in its grip as water raced down the passage. Try as they might, the men were unable to close the flood door, but at least they managed to escape. Two days later the best the pumps could do was to hold the water level in the Old Shaft at 40 m (130 ft.).

The railroad company put in another call to Lambert. This time, it took the diver just two tries—one using Fleuss's rebreathing gear and the other using standard diving equipment—to reach the flood door and shut it. Less than a week later, the tunnel was clear and the Great Spring was confined again.

There's no doubt that Alexander Lambert played an important, though unusual, role in the building of the Severn tunnel. Without him, it probably never would have opened to traffic when it did in 1886—almost 14 years after Great Western started building. The tunnel is still in use, although few lumps of coal pass through it today.

The work that Lambert did in the tunnel also contributed to diving technology. He put the Fleuss rebreather through its first set of heavy-duty tests. The invention was gradually improved, and formed a basis for developing the submarine escape equipment used by the Royal Navy in World War I.

As for the Great Spring, it was eventually turned to good use. Engineers gave up trying to contain it and sank a special shaft to help pump the water to the surface. Even today, the spring produces fine-quality water in such volumes that it supplies a paper mill, a brewery, a steelworks—and an entire community.

Eleven people, including a tiny baby girl, huddled together in an abandoned store in East Berlin. Quietly...nervously...they took turns wriggling through the entrance to a tunnel that ran beneath the streets and under a wall bordering the city. The passageway was damp, dark, and narrow—no wider than an airplane seat. Still, the baby's mother managed to bring the infant by towing her in a cradlelike sled built for the escape.

Creeping through the tunnel, the group hardly dared to breathe. With each passing second, they feared the baby might cry and attract the attention of police officers patrolling directly overhead. But they needn't have worried. The mother had given the baby a mild sleeping pill, and the infant dozed the whole trip through the tunnel. All 11 escapees emerged safely in the basement of a small café in West Berlin. They were free!

Such escapes were frequent after the East Germans shocked the world in 1961 by building a wall between East and West Berlin. Not that they were the first people ever to raise a wall to stop border-crossers. Throughout history, castles and forts in many countries used walls to protect their residents; China constructed the world's longest wall to defend its people from northern invaders. But the wall that East Germany erected

Germany and Berlin
when the Wall Appeared

Denmark

West
Berlin

East
Berlin

Netherlands

East
Germany

Poland

Belgium

West
Germany

Czechoslovakia

France

Switzerland

Austria

imprisoned the country's own citizens. No wonder so many tried to escape.

A Country Divided

At the end of World War II, Germany was defeated and occupied by the victors. At first, the country was divided into four zones of occupation. Then in 1949, the American, British, and French zones united to form the country of West Germany, under a democratic government. The Soviet-occupied zone became East Germany, under a Communist government (see map).

Germany's capital city of Berlin, completely surrounded by East Germany, was also split in two. West Berlin became a West German city, while East Berlin became the capital of East Germany.

Berliners, however, didn't think of themselves as "East" or "West" people. They were simply Berliners. As they went to work, attended school, visited friends, or bought groceries, many of them crossed the city border daily. West Berlin offered people more opportunities and more freedom. Like the rest of West Germany, it had recovered from the war more quickly than East Germany.

During the years that followed the split, life in East Germany grew tougher, and control of its border tighter. In 1952, the government posted guards along the country's entire frontier. After that, the only easy way to leave the country was through East Berlin. There, dissatisfied East Germans could pose as commuters, hop on a subway train, and enter West Berlin. They could either stay there permanently or fly into the rest of West Germany. And many did.

Between 1945 and 1961, more than 3 million people, including thousands of East Germany's most highly trained technicians and professionals, fled the country. In one day—August 11, 1961—more than 4,000 people crossed into West Berlin. The East German government and the Soviet authorities were desperate to stop the flow.

Wall of Shame

Two days later, they made their move. At around 2:00 a.m., armed forces started digging trenches and erecting a barrier of barbed wire along the border between East and West Berlin. Soldiers and police officers with tanks, rifles, and tear gas stood guard. They allowed no one to cross into West Berlin without permission—something out of the reach of most East Germans.

Imagine the amazement and horror of Berliners when they awoke that morning. Without warning, their city had been physically chopped into two. For more than 50,000 people, the ugly barrier stood between home and work, suddenly putting them out of the jobs they needed to support themselves and their families. Many couldn't find new work; others grabbed whatever they could. Skilled mechanics worked as laborers. Professional teachers spent their days delivering parcels.

The Berlin Wall also forced more than 1,200 children who had been studying in West Berlin to find spaces in East Berlin schools. Not all of them could. Some ended up working in factories instead of going to classes.

Most heartbreaking of all were the people the wall held apart. There were children who couldn't see their grandparents, friends who couldn't visit one another, and sweethearts who couldn't marry. Before long, even phone calls between East and West Berlin were banned, and letters that passed between them were checked and censored.

To make matters worse, troops began adding concrete slabs to the barrier. Up and up—on and on—the wall grew. As the weeks went by, it became taller, longer, and stronger. In places, builders worked so quickly that they dripped cement down the sides. Berliners called the drips "tears," and named the barricade the "Wall of Shame."

And what a shame it was. Zigzagging for about 45 km (28 mi.) between the cities, the Berlin Wall split streets in half, divided neighborhoods, and sliced through the middle of parks and cemeteries. It stood 3 m (10 ft.) high in many spots and 6 m (20 ft.) in others. In some places, it was topped with sharp chunks of jagged glass and barbed wire.

Along busy sections of the city, troops built observation towers close to the wall. They blocked bridges with sandbags and erected additional concrete barriers near border-crossing points to help prevent escapes.

By August 29, 1961, East Germans were not allowed to stand within 90 m (300 ft.) of the wall without running the risk of being arrested or shot. If they gathered just to wave at friends and relatives who climbed ladders in West Berlin to see them, the police tossed tear gas into the crowds.

Soon, guards along the Berlin Wall became more heavily armed, and contact between East and West fell even more. Police spot-checked homes to see if any radios were tuned to West Berlin stations—an offence that was punishable by prison.

During the first weeks after the Berlin Wall appeared, many

people managed to escape to West Berlin. By ones or twos, they climbed over the wall, leapt from buildings that stood close to it, or hid inside vehicles that were allowed to cross the border. But the only way that families or larger groups could flee together was by sneaking out, like rats, through tunnels.

Heading Underground

Beneath the original capital of Berlin lay a sprawling sewer system that connected streets from one end of the city to the other. For hundreds of East Germans, these pipes formed a vast network of freedom tunnels.

Still, the pipes were far from easy routes to take. Some were large enough to allow adults to walk stooped over, but others were so small there was barely room to crawl. Parts of the sewer system drained rainwater from the streets and filled up suddenly during storms. Other sections carried thick streams of waste that escapees had to wade through. The wastes gave off poisonous gases that made breathing difficult—if not impossible. And the metal traps used to screen the wastes in pipes were serious barriers to travel. Only where there was enough space beneath the traps—or where they could be sawed off— were escapees able to wriggle under them.

Another hazard was the police force, who patrolled the streets constantly. Any coughing or talking drew officers to manholes, into which they would toss tear gas.

Students of the Sewers

Most of the successful sewer escapes were directed by students from West Berlin's Free University and Institute of Technology.

They had seen the wall cut off fellow students from their education and were determined to help them and their families get out of East Berlin.

The students prepared themselves well. They studied maps of the sewer system and picked out the safest, most direct routes. They chose manholes on streets close to the wall to act as tunnel entrances.

On dark nights, one of the students would raise a manhole cover for East Berlin families who were prepared to escape. Once they were safely inside the sewer system, other students would shepherd them through. The first student would remain to replace the cover—escapees were often so nervous they'd neglect to do it themselves. That same student would arrange for the next group of escapees to assemble, then leave for West Germany with them. Another recruit remained to cover the manhole and prepare more escapees.

Police did their best to stop the sewer breakouts. They set up stronger barricades and installed more screens in the pipes. And they considered themselves successful when dead bodies began to pile up in the sewer system.

One and a half years after the Berlin Wall went up, however, two men pulled off an amazing escape by breaking through the sewer barricades with strong metal cutters. A pair of teenagers happened to spot them entering the system through a manhole and followed the men. Together, the four of them gasped their way through the gas-filled tunnels.

When they could go no farther, they tried exiting through a manhole. But it was winter, and the cover was frozen shut. The men set fire to a handkerchief and attracted passersby with the smoke. Luckily, the four had traveled just far enough to have reached a street in West Berlin. The path they created through the sewer system provided a route to the West for more escapees before police found it and sealed it up.

Digging Out

Many East Germans who fled underground to West Berlin used tunnels built especially for the purpose. Some simply dug their own way out. Three factory employees spent a long weekend burrowing from their workplace on the border. As soon as their fellow workers had left for the short holiday, the men hid themselves inside the factory. They tunneled night and day, not even stopping to eat or sleep. Two of the men dug with spoons and small shovels, while the third carted pail after pail of dirt back to the factory. It was a desperate race against the clock, but in the final hours, all three reached West Berlin.

One of the most well-known escape artists was an East German engraver, named Wolfgang Fuchs. He had been helped by friends to cross the border and was determined to rescue others. Fuchs returned to East Berlin several times to sneak people into the West. On one escape, he organized a group to dig a tunnel between a former West Berlin bakery and an East Berlin outhouse. He used the tunnel to move 57 people safely to the West before East German soldiers closed it down.

Fuchs and others like him risked a lot to help escapees. The penalty for encouraging people to leave East Germany, or merely praising life elsewhere, was several years in jail. Anyone caught helping someone skip the country could be killed. One West

Berliner who guided 35 people to an escape tunnel was shot on the spot when police turned up and fired into the passageway.

Team Operations

None of this stopped West Berlin university students from rolling up their sleeves and building tunnels to freedom. And they got the help of volunteers from other countries, such as Sweden, Italy, Israel, the United Kingdom, and the United States. Besides diggers, there were engineers who designed the passageways, lookouts who watched for police, and couriers who selected the best entries and prepared the escapees.

The engineers usually started a tunnel close to the wall on the West Berlin side. They picked a spot that East German patrols couldn't see well and one that might lead to sandy soil, which was easy to dig. If a tunnel opening had to be created through a basement wall, diggers chipped away patiently with plain hammers and chisels. Electric drills made far too much noise, attracting the attention of police.

Most passages ran beneath city streets, so the engineers had to figure out how and where to support the weight of the pavement and vehicles. To avoid running into underground pipes and cables, they often told diggers to burrow down at least 5 m (16 ft.).

The diggers worked long shifts, usually in darkness. Other members of their team hauled and dumped loads of sand and rock. Day by day, a tunnel might grow 3.5 to 5 m (12 to 16 ft.). It was often no less than 90 m (300 ft.) long before it was done.

While they worked, the diggers faced risks from floods and cave-ins. They often found it hard to breathe. Now and then a pole or fencepost broke through a tunnel roof and struck them. Even after they finished their shifts, they weren't free of danger. The layer of sand and mud that coated their clothes told the tale of what they'd been up to.

Of course, it was much easier to enter East Berlin than it was to leave it. Foreign students and others with no close connections to East Germans sometimes got permission to enter East Berlin. Then they worked as couriers for the tunnel teams.

One of their jobs was to scout out suitable places for entrances on that side of the wall. The best sites tended to be in sheds or basements close enough to the wall that the tunnels didn't need to be too long—but far enough away that escapees wouldn't be within range of the guards' guns. Finding the right spots was no easy task, especially after East German officials began destroying many of the abandoned buildings near the wall.

Another of the couriers' duties was to let East German students and families know the place and time for their escape. The escapees were often told the secret arrangements just 15 minutes ahead. If they discovered the schedule much earlier, they could be tempted to sell their cars or say goodbye to friends—accidentally revealing the escape plan. The short notice meant that couriers had to speed around East Berlin to reach everyone. Some people missed their chance to flee just because they couldn't be found.

Escape times were usually staggered so people didn't attract attention by gathering in large groups. As many as 30 might leave through a single tunnel during an evening.

The escapees occasionally created problems for the courier. No matter what they'd been told, some tried to take too much with them. They'd arrive with pets or large suitcases that slowed movement through the tunnels. Some even tried to bring extra people with them. And they'd wear clothing that wasn't appropriate—high heels that clattered noisily on the pavement or fur coats that made crawling through tunnels very difficult.

Excited and fearful, escapees occasionally forgot to whisper in the tunnels, and they often failed to stifle groans and cries—or to quiet their children—when they heard officers nearby. The danger of being discovered was ever present. "I was terrified they would shoot me in the back," said one East German who escaped through a tunnel 150 m (500 ft.) long.

If the students were lucky, the same tunnel might be used as many as five times or more. Once the police or soldiers found it, however, it was sealed over or blown up. And the students would start tunneling all over again.

Lights, Camera, Money

As the police and armed forces grew more aware of escapes, the students had to set up tunnel entrances farther from the wall. That meant longer, more expensive passages, and raising money for the additional materials became a problem. Sympathetic donors and escapees contributed funds, and the media sometimes paid for news stories. But as it turned out, that wasn't always a good thing.

In 1962, an American TV company bought the right to make a documentary about one of the students' tunnels. With the funds, the team set out to build an elaborate underpass that could be used many times, perhaps by hundreds of East Germans.

Starting from a house in West Berlin, diggers tunneled through sand for roughly 110 m (360 ft.) and exited in the basement of an apartment building. The students worked on the passage for months, erecting supports for the roof and walls and installing electric lights, ventilation, an alarm system, even phone lines for emergencies. To haul out the sand, they set up a small cart that ran on rails.

Throughout the building of the tunnel, a TV cameraman filmed the team's efforts. On the day of the escape, he joined 29 East German adults and children and headed underground. But along the way, water pipes started leaking into the passage, and walls began to collapse. As frightened as they were, everyone carried on to West Berlin. Amazingly, another 33 people waded and swam their way through the tunnel later that same day.

The students were frustrated by the short life of their tunnel. What's worse, they were shocked that the documentary of their operations would be shown on TV much sooner than they had expected. They feared it would put their lives—and those of others in East Berlin—at risk and help the police catch similar teams at work. "It never occurred to me they'd put the program on the air there and then," said one of the students. "But that's what they did." Despite the protests, the film was broadcast shortly after the escape while other tunnels were being built.

Into the Grave

Still, the university students carried on, and tales of their bravery and exploits grew. Of the many escapes they engineered, one of the most imaginative had people vanishing through a grave! A tunnel-building team had dug a passage that ran 14 m (46 ft.) from a West Berlin shed to an East Berlin cemetery. It emerged in a fake grave with a removable, sod-covered top.

Because the cemetery bordered the Berlin Wall, it was closely guarded by the police. Officers watched all visitors who came to mourn their loved ones, including escapees who brought flowers to the special "grave."

The students posted a lookout on the roof of the shed that was the tunnel exit. From there, the lookout could watch as the officers passed the grave on their rounds. As soon as they had walked by, the lookout signaled a second student inside the shed. That student pulled a rope connected through the tunnel to the leg of a third student hidden in the grave. A sharp tug meant, "All's clear." That student then slid back the grass-covered grave top, stuck out a hand, and silently gestured to the gathered "mourners." In seconds, they disappeared underground and slid the top back in place.

More than 150 people in several small groups reached West Berlin through that tunnel. Others might have escaped the same way, but a nervous young mother, fleeing with her baby, accidentally tipped off the police. She had abandoned her child's stroller near the grave.

Down Came the Wall

The hated Berlin Wall imprisoned East Germans for 28 long years. But during that time, Soviet control of the country slowly weakened and relations between East and West gradually improved. On November 9, 1989, the border that had kept

Germany divided finally opened up. East Germans poured freely into West Berlin, and their celebrations lasted for days.

Berlin's Wall of Shame soon fell, and souvenir hunters, known as "wall woodpeckers," carted it away in chunks. "This living in a cage is over!" yelled one East German joyfully.

The following year, the countries of East and West Germany became one again, and the cities of East and West Berlin reunited to form the capital.

The Great Bank Robbery

It must have been a strange sight: rubber dinghies, beach mattresses, and inner tubes, all strung together and floating through a sewer. In the early hours of July 19, 1976, a gang of thieves was using this oddball train to haul piles of gold, jewelry, and cash from a vault. The main branch of the Société Générale bank in Nice, France, had just been robbed of $10–$12 million—one of the biggest booties in the history of bank burglaries!

Not that the vault was easy to break into. Sitting below ground level, it was shielded from the rest of the bank by a pair of locked steel doors set in solid walls of concrete. Behind them was another locked steel door about 1 m (3 ft.) thick and weighing 18 t (20 tons). So solid was this door that the bank didn't think it was necessary to install an electronic alarm system. Its insurance company agreed. On weekends, there wasn't even a nighttime security guard.

Metal grates divided the vault into three rooms: a treasury room, a safe-deposit room, and a night safe. The bank kept its cash and gold bars in the treasury room. Clients stored their valuables in 4,000 double-locked boxes in the safe-deposit room. Businesses deposited cash in the night safe after bank hours. Shoved in bags through an opening at the street above, the money slid down a chute directly into the safe.

The Société Générale bank served many of the wealthy retired people of Nice, a popular resort city. A number of these well-off people preferred keeping their fortunes in solid gold, cash, and jewelry rather than in stocks and bonds. They locked their riches in safe-deposit boxes in large banks that appeared to be very secure. But on one hot Monday in July, they discovered that even the strongest of vaults wasn't enough to keep out thieves.

The question was: Who could have possibly walked away with a such a huge chunk of the wealth stashed in the Société Générale—just 180 m (590 ft.) from police headquarters—and how?

The Mastermind

Meet Albert Spaggiari of France. As a teenager, he had enroled in the army to gain military training and experience, but in 1954, when he was only 22, he was jailed for theft. A few years later, he joined a terrorist group called the *Organisation Armée Secrète* (OAS), or Secret Army Organization, which tried to assassinate the president of France in the early 1960s. Some of their members robbed banks to support the organization's activities.

In 1962, Spaggiari was jailed again, this time for his work with the OAS. But he appears to have had nothing to do with the Société Générale bank until 1974, when he rented a safe-deposit box there. He later claimed that that was when he first got the idea to break into the vault.

Spaggiari planned the robbery very carefully. He researched

the bank and its neighborhood, formed the team he would need, and gathered materials and equipment to set up the robbery. He conducted the whole operation with military efficiency. From what investigators and judges were able to piece together, here's what likely happened.

The Plan

According to bank records, Spaggiari legally entered the vault in the Société Générale only twice. The second time was in January 1975. Like all clients with safe-deposit boxes, he had to sign a log on entering. Besides using the opportunity to check out the vault, he might have also picked up useful information—such as the weight of the big metal safe-deposit cabinets—from a bank employee.

At Nice's town hall, Spaggiari announced that he planned to build an underground nightclub, so helpful staff handed him detailed drawings of the city's sewer system. He used them to plot a route through the system to the street nearest the bank (see diagram).

The route he chose began on a wide underground road along the pipes that carried the winter flow of the Paillon River through Nice. Only sewer workers used the road, when they checked the drainage system.

One entrance to the road was through an underground parking lot and a siphon room for measuring rainfall. Spaggiari discovered that security cameras guarded both the parking lot and the door to the siphon room. But he figured he could use that entrance safely if he parked a car in front of the door, blocking the camera's view.

Bank Robbers' Route

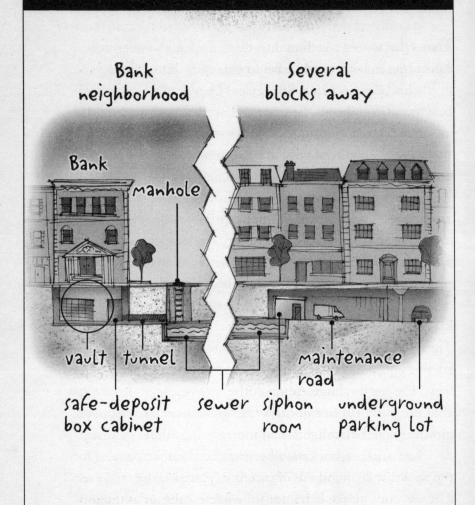

Bank neighborhood

Several blocks away

Bank

manhole

vault tunnel

maintenance road

safe-deposit box cabinet

sewer

siphon room

underground parking lot

In a street very near the Société Générale was a manhole that opened into the sewer system. Convenient—but risky—for a bank robber to use. Still, Spaggiari thought that it would be handy for moving heavy equipment underground.

While these ready-made tunnels, the sewer pipes, would get Spaggiari close to the bank, his plans called for one more tunnel that would take him directly to the bank's underground vault. That one he would have to create for himself.

With plans in place, Spaggiari set up a team of tunnel-builders and lookouts, later known as the "Sewer Rats." He knew that digging a tunnel from the sewer system to the vault would be no small task. For that, he needed an expert—so he arranged to spring the man he wanted out of jail!

So complete was his team of about 15 men that it included a doctor who would be on call in case of any emergency during the robbery. Spaggiari also arranged for a jeweler who would join the team inside the vault and select the most valuable gems—the ones really worth stealing.

Gathering the Goods

The first task for the Sewer Rats was to gather all the material and equipment needed to build the tunnel and rob the bank. The list was huge. Among other items, it included inflatable dinghies, rubber boots, waterproof overalls, raincoats, gloves, goggles, flashlights, hammers, drills, chisels, gas cylinders, blowtorches, buckets, wheelbarrows, lumber, cement for the tunnel walls, hundreds of meters of electric cable, and even a heavy-duty smoke extractor to help clear the air as the robbers tunneled into the vault.

The gang had to shop cautiously for supplies so that they didn't draw attention to themselves. For instance, they couldn't buy large amounts of anything at one place. That meant going to stores all over Nice and other cities in France. Sometimes they had to shop in different western European countries, such as Italy and Belgium.

The shops that the gang favored were large department stores where they were less likely to be noticed or remembered later. They chose common brands of products, which would be harder for the police to trace. Although they were thieves, they didn't want to endanger their planned bank heist by stealing the small stuff. Generally—though not always—they paid for the things they took.

As their supplies mounted, the gang needed a place to store them. Spaggiari found an empty, isolated mansion a short distance from Nice.

Building the Tunnel

During spring, the Sewer Rats got busy constructing the tunnel to the bank. It had to reach 7 m (23 ft.) from the sewer to the vault through soil that was unstable. They labored hard for about two months to complete it.

Teams took turns digging the passage. As planned, they used a car to block the view of the security camera near the siphon room door in the underground parking lot. Then a truck carrying tunnelers and equipment slipped in behind the car. The team hauled tools and materials through the siphon room to the underground road. Then they waded through the sewers, floating their equipment on inflatables, such as rubber dinghies, for hundreds of meters through the system.

In each team, two men with picks and shovels chipped and dug, while another hauled away the waste and dumped it in a dead-end pipe in the sewer system. The chief tunnel builder moved in next, propping the roof up with lumber and cementing the walls.

Working inside the tunnel was often so difficult that the men could only manage 10-minute stretches with 10-minute breaks in between. But the smoke extractor that Spaggiari brought in helped clear the air and cool the tunnel.

Power to run equipment such as drills came from a light socket in the underground parking lot. The Sewer Rats ran an electric cable through the siphon room and along the ceiling of the sewer to their tunnel.

In case city workers happened to come across the tunnel during the daytime, the Rats took pains to make it look as if it belonged. They created a narrow entrance, and painted the tunnel's concrete walls to match the color of the sewer system. These precautions proved especially valuable on July 10 when Giscard d'Estaing, the president of France at the time, visited Nice. Security forces were making the city safe for his arrival, and even checking the sewers for explosives.

Spaggiari set up his own security force while the tunnel was being constructed. He posted a sentry near the street entrance to the underground parking lot. If necessary, the man would charge through the siphon room to alert a messenger. In turn, the messenger would race to the sewer along the underground road and blow a whistle. As well, a motorcycle sentry was stationed about 2 km (1.2 mi.) away at another entrance to the underground road. If he spotted anything suspicious, he would drive down the road, then race to the sewer on foot to sound the whistle.

Breaking Through

It was early in July when the tunnelers first hit the vault's thick concrete wall. They chipped about halfway through it and finished shoring up the tunnel. Then they were ready for the final push—breaking through the wall and into the vault. Of course, that would all have to be done on a single weekend, when the bank was closed. The Sewer Rats decided to make their move on the evening of Friday, July 16.

Trying not to attract any attention, one group of robbers moved into the sewer system through the entrance to the underground road where the motorcycle sentry was stationed. The others came in through the underground parking lot and loaded equipment onto inflatables. As soon as they had hauled a load through the sewer to the tunnel, they headed back to the parking lot for more stuff. In all, they transferred about a ton of goods.

Inside the tunnel, they made a "rug" out of rope so they could lug their supplies along the floor with less effort. But the really heavy equipment—a hydraulic lever and several gas cylinders—would have to come in later through the manhole.

The gang spent the entire night drilling, hammering, chiseling, and shoveling in the heat and smoke of the tunnel. Amazingly, even the loud noise of their jackhammers could not be heard on the street above. Spaggiari checked to make sure.

By the Saturday morning, the men were exhausted. Only

the knowledge of the treasure that lay inside the vault kept them going the rest of the day. It was late afternoon before they broke through the concrete wall, and it took another five hours of muscle and sweat before they made a hole big enough for them to pass through. Then the men used blowtorches to cut the steel bars imbedded in the wall.

The next obstacle was a heavy metal cabinet that held a raft of safe-deposit boxes. It stood with its back pressed to the concrete wall the gang had just cracked. Sliding that weight of several tons out of the way called for the hydraulic lift.

At a signal from the tunnel crew, the lookout near the entrance to the underground parking lot drove to a waiting van, honking as it passed. The van looked just like ones used by an electric company. Two gang members pulled on electric company uniforms and drove the van to the manhole near the bank. At that point, they were less than 3 m (10 ft.) from the underground tunnel.

Like a company work crew, the men set out a blue light and a sign that read, "Danger: Men at Work." Then they passed the equipment to the men in the sewer, gathered up the light and the sign, and disappeared—all within minutes.

With the help of the hydraulic lift, the Sewer Rats moved the huge metal cabinet just enough to allow a man to slip past it. Spaggiari was the first to enter the vault. It was early Sunday morning.

Inside the Vault

The first thing the thieves did was to weld the vault's door shut from the inside—in case some bank employee tried to enter during the weekend. Then they sealed openings, such as air vents, so that no light or sound could escape and give them away. Now all they had to do was help themselves to the contents of the vault.

Working furiously, the Sewer Rats broke into 317 of the 4,000 safe-deposit boxes, grabbing gold, cash, and precious jewels. They cut through the metal door to the treasury room and snatched all the bank's reserves of gold and cash. They hacked into the night safe for the money that businesses had deposited since the bank closed on Friday. While they were there, an additional $175,000 from a casino dropped down the chute right into the waiting arms of the thieves!

The gang had labored a day and a half in the tunnel without eating or drinking much of anything. Inside the vault, they stopped to feast on hot soup (they'd brought a portable stove with them), fine sausages, cheese, fruit, dates, and wine. Then they returned to their looting, wrapping gold bars in paper and packing cash and jewels away in plastic bags. By early Monday morning, it was time to flee the bank, so they piled their treasure onto the inflatables and took off through the sewers.

If they could have, the gang might have hauled away more. The value of what they left lying on the floor of the vault was close to $2 million. The thieves also abandoned boxes of cigars, bottles of wine, and other leftovers from their feast, as well as many of the tools and equipment they had been using.

On the wall, someone had taken time to draw a Celtic cross, the symbol of an illegal organization operating in France. Beside it was this message: *Sans armes, sans haine, et sans violence.* (Without guns, without hatred, and without violence.)

The Investigation

What the Sewer Rats DIDN'T leave behind was a clue of any kind. The police found none of their fingerprints anywhere. After the gang's cautious shopping trips, the materials and equipment they abandoned left no useful trails to follow. And the urine and excrement that each robber created during the full weekend in the vault had been mixed with the urine and excrement of the others. The waste was untraceable to any single person.

However, not all the Sewer Rats were as clever as Albert Spaggiari, and some made mistakes following the robbery. For instance, one of them insisted on taking his share of the gold and selling it at a higher price than Spaggiari had arranged with a special dealer. The sale eventually caught the attention of the police. By fall, two of the Rats had been arrested and tricked into fingering Spaggiari as the ringleader of the Société Générale bank robbery.

On October 27, 1976, the police picked up Spaggiari, questioning him for 37 hours, nonstop. Finally, he made a bargain: He would confess to the robbery in exchange for protection for his wife. She would not be picked up and questioned about any possible involvement in the crime.

That week, Spaggiari began making a long series of court appearances before a judge. He seemed to enjoy the attention. At each session, he talked up a storm. He described how his team created the tunnel and set up the robbery through the sewer system. He bragged and he exaggerated. Sometimes, he lied. He also claimed that his share of the robbery went to help people in other countries. But he didn't say one word that would help police identify the rest of the gang or recover the stolen goods.

The Escape

On March 10, 1977, Spaggiari—well dressed as usual—arrived at the courthouse for his 20th appearance. The police removed his handcuffs and locked him inside a room with his lawyer, the judge, and the person who was recording his testimony. After asking several questions, the judge requested a detailed plan of the robbery, which Spaggiari had promised to provide that week.

Spaggiari passed the judge a sheet of paper covered with drawings, symbols, and descriptions. The judge couldn't understand it, so Spaggiari walked around his desk to point out something—then jumped out of the second-story window. He landed on a ledge above a side door to the courthouse. From there, he leapt to the roof of a parked car, then down to the street. Waiting for him was a motorcycle rider, raring to go. Together, they took off, Spaggiari holding up his fingers in a "V" for victory sign.

Almost instantly, the police were in hot pursuit. Travel out of Nice was blocked. The French border was closed. But Spaggiari simply disappeared.

Nine days later, the Organisation Armée Secrète declared he was out of the country. But Spaggiari kept in touch with what was happening back home. When a Nice newspaper ran a story about the damages to the roof of the car he had dropped down on, he sent the owner an apology and cash to pay for the repairs.

In the End

Most of the Sewer Rats got away with their crime and their share of the goods from the robbery. Only about $200,000 worth of loot was ever recovered. What's more, the total stolen might have been greater than what was reported. Contents of safe-deposit boxes are confidential, and some are used by people to hide their riches from tax collectors.

As for Albert Spaggiari, he likely spent most of the rest of his life in South America, where he was suspected of working with terrorists. In his absence from France, he was convicted of robbing the Société Générale bank in Nice in what the French called *le fric-frac du siècle*—the burglary of the century. He was sentenced to life in prison.

Spaggiari was also named as a suspect in two similar robberies in France: one of a Paris branch of Société Générale in 1976 and another in Marseille in 1987. Whatever his brilliant, though criminal, career involved, Albert Spaggiari died in 1989, still remembered as the kingpin of the tunneling Sewer Rats.

Index

About the Author

Diane Swanson grew up in Diane Swanson grew up in Lethbridge, Alberta, where she collected rocks, watched insects, went swimming, ate ice cream cones, and wrote stories of all kinds. Now a full-time author, Diane has made a career of writing exciting and informative non-fiction books for kids. She is the author of *Nibbling on Einstein's Brain* and more than 50 other books for children. These award-winning books have earned the attention of the B.C. Award, the Orbis Pictus Award for Outstanding Nonfiction for Children, the Mr. Christie's Book Award, the B.C. Book Prize, the Red Cedar Award, the Silver Birch Award, and many more.

Diane now lives in Victoria, B.C., with her family. When not writing or doing research on something fascinating, she often speaks about fascinating things at schools and conferences.